SUNSET GRATITUDE

365 HOPEFUL MEDITATIONS
FOR PEACEFUL AND REFLECTIVE
EVENINGS ALL YEAR LONG

EMILY SILVA

ROCK
POINT

Dedication

For Nate, who held a candle of hope during my dark days of grief.

For those sitting in the waiting room of life searching for hope to return after grief has come to visit.

Introduction

GOOD EVENING. Gratitude has been a running theme in my life. For over a decade, I've been sharing and writing about gratitude in workshops and books. Practicing gratitude can change your life, which is why it's touched on often throughout these pages.

The inspiration for this book was finding hope after a period of grief. There are many things that can cause one to grieve and hope can feel out of reach during those times.

Sunsets symbolize an ending. When things end, it can feel hard to accept and surrender to what is. Letting go is rarely easy and I wanted these passages to be gentle reminders that it's okay to take your time.

Sunsets also remind us that another day is coming. When one thing ends, there is space for something else to arrive. Endings aren't always bad, as they can often lead to something beautiful.

I finished the first draft of this book when the moon was full. I completed the first book of this series, *Moonlight Gratitude*, under a full moon as well. If it wasn't for the sunset, we'd never be able to marvel at the moon.

The sun and moon are beautiful reminders of the cyclical nature of life. There is always something beginning and ending; rising and setting.

Like my previous books, you can read each day's passage in chronological order, or open to any page whenever you need hope or inspiration. You will also find affirmations at the beginning of each month to repeat to yourself whenever you need them.

May these words provide comfort and hope during life's struggles and help you feel like you're not alone.

January 1

AS YOU WIND DOWN on the first day of the year, repeat these affirmations to yourself: *I am grateful for all the goodness in my life. I open my hands to receive the goodness that's on its way to me with gratitude, joy, and worthiness. I let go of all the things I cling to in fear of losing them. What is meant to be will stay. I release what's meant to leave. I recognize all the goodness that is already in my life with reverence. I am worthy of wonderful and beautiful things.*

January 2

THE SUN SETS, PAINTING THE SKY with beautiful hues.
Sunsets are a reminder of the cyclical nature of life. As
the earth rotates around the sun, we are offered different
perspectives of light. Every day we have the chance to
appreciate the colors of twilight right before the darkness
of night. When we take the time to appreciate the cycles in
life, we can see that nothing is permanent and we can hold
out hope for better days ahead.

———

January 3

THERE ARE TIMES WHEN everything seems to be
working against us. In these periods, gratitude can be
hard to come by, and yet, it is when the practice is most
important. Gratitude is like a healing balm for our anxious
hearts. By taking a few moments to be grateful, we remind
our hearts that not all is lost and we allow our worries to
fade. Take a moment to pause and offer thanks for one good
thing that's in your life.

January 4

SPACE CONTINUES TO BE EXPLORED and we are fortunate to be witnesses to the new discoveries. The birth of stars, Technicolor galaxies, and the intricacies of planets we grew up seeing as drawings on a page are now vibrant images for us to appreciate. There is always more to learn and discover. When you think you know everything about a person or situation, challenge yourself to go deeper. The deeper we go, the more open we can be to astonishment.

January 5

TENSION IS AN INVITATION TO SOFTEN. When moments of contraction occur, fear is speaking louder than hope. Moving from fear to a place of hope takes time. Be patient with the process. With awareness we can slowly lower fear's volume and welcome calm. Eventually the noise quiets down and the energy feels more expansive. Our hearts can soften into the space we create when we release the tension that keeps us tight. Hope will bloom where fear once spoke.

January 6

JUDGMENT CREATES SEPARATION. When we judge another, we position our hearts away from them. Trying to understand and turning toward each other helps keep judgment at bay. Sometimes what we are judging in others reflects something that we judge about ourselves. See judgment as an invitation for healing. The next time you notice your inner judge holding court, turn inward and offer yourself compassion, then extend it toward the person you are judging. From here, understanding and compassion can take root.

———

January 7

WHEN A TREE FALLS DOWN, it offers nourishment to the forest floor. There is a richness within the tree as it provides sustenance and shelter to the understory of the forest. The same can be true when we fall. Failure doesn't mean we are not valuable. Failure is a redirection to the path we are meant to be on. Embracing the cycles of growth, decay, and rebirth can help us move forward during times of breakdown. Your life is full of value.

January 8

THE UNIVERSE HEARS OUR deepest desires. What we long for can occupy our minds, causing tension to well up. When we feel anxious, it's natural to want to do something to feel in control. But control is the opposite of trust. Holding something with a tight grip doesn't allow miracles to take place. Release your grasp, trusting that life is happening for you. It's okay to let go. The universe is kind and loving. Everything is happening as it needs to.

———

January 9

SOME DAYS FEEL IMPOSSIBLE to get through. It can feel like anything and everything falls apart. Solutions seem to be elusive, keeping order at bay. Days like these feel like a pressure cooker of stress. When things are stuck, pressure can build, sometimes causing panic. Stress and anxiety can feel like stuck energy within. When your day feels impossible, stop and move. Dance, walk, run, stretch. The problems may not go away, but the pressure can move through you. Movement is a sacred release of the tension within.

January 10

NOT ALL ROADS ARE SMOOTH, but eventually the destination is reached. If you're traveling on a bumpier road in life, notice the resilience and wisdom you are gaining and reach out to ask for help if needed. Often others aren't aware of our needs. Sometimes being vulnerable and honest about our situation can enlighten our loved ones in ways they can be there for us. When we state our needs, we open up to the support we desire.

———————

January 11

A BEAR HIBERNATES DURING THE WINTER after months of preparation. It doesn't ask permission; instinct drives it to hibernate. Guided by intuition, it survives. When you feel the inner stirrings of longing, notice how your body responds. Don't quell the true yearnings of your soul or allow guilt to keep you from your needs. When we ignore our intuition, we can neglect our basic needs. Listen to your intuition; you are worthy of care and the desires of your heart.

January 12

THE PERSPECTIVE WE CHOOSE generates the energy
we feel. Have you ever noticed how choosing a different
thought can shift the way you feel? Instead of dreading the
week, think of the opportunities and connections ahead. Let
go of thoughts that can send you into a spiral and replace
them with ones that are uplifting or more neutral. It's a
lovely way to welcome love and peace where frustration
tends to take root. When you feel your energy needs a shift,
observe your thoughts to make room for growth.

January 13

IT'S FUTILE TO RESIST CHANGE as it's always occurring.
Think of the seasons and stages of life. Everything
is constantly transitioning and it's important to slow
down when we feel tension rising within. Tension is the
gateway to resistance and change. When you feel tension,
understand that your body is trying to tell you something.
Unless you slow down to listen, you can miss or delay these
important messages. Slowing down allows change to occur
and reveals answers that are key to moving forward.

January 14

THERE ARE TREES THAT HAVE SURVIVED for hundreds of years. They've stood magnificently during droughts, frosts, and wildfires. As the years pass, their circumferences expand, adding rings inside their trunks. Although the trees may reveal scars, they still continue to tower over the forest below, providing nature's cathedral for those willing to explore. Be like a tree and reach for the sky, even after painful experiences. New dreams can sprout through hardships. Growing through pain cultivates reverence and resilience.

———

January 15

LIVING IN A SPACE THAT FEELS in-between is difficult, especially if it seems like it's lasting forever. If you're in a liminal space, look for something to be grateful for. Even the small moments of gratitude change perspectives. Surrender all the desires that keep your heart from being present. What is meant for you will happen. Sometimes it shows up when we least expect it. Releasing the grasp around expectations opens our hands to receive what's meant to be.

January 16

OUR SOUL WORK IS NEVER COMPLETED because we are ever evolving. Just as the sun sets each day, joys and sorrows come and go. During times of struggle, soulful practices can be supportive. When you feel like life is amazing, keep meditating, journaling, and praying. Show up and listen to your intuition. It's during these times that we strengthen our spiritual muscles, because when something happens, we will use the muscle memory to help get us through the hard times.

———

January 17

ON THE BEACH, TWO WAVES are about to collide. They are both part of a big ocean. After the collision, they recede back into the vast sea. There will always be opposition in life. With so much division, fear, and confusion milling about, we have a choice to live life from a place of anger and opposition or with love and healing. We all need love and healing. Choose to love. Love brings healing. Healing brings love. Love brings us together like waves on the shore.

January 18

AT THE DAY'S END, IT'S EASY to want to check out. Taking some time to transition from a full day is an act of self-care and compassion. Before we can be present, our nervous systems need a period of time to decompress from the pressures of the day. Notice when you feel guilty for taking moments to yourself. Even a few moments to readjust can shift the energy from distracted to present. Remember that caring for yourself helps you to be more present with loved ones.

———

January 19

WHEN THE SUN SETS over the ocean, it looks as if the sea is tucking it in for the night. As the sun continues to dip below the horizon, the sky fills with a variety of hues in orange, rose, and lavender. Each color gradually changes into the dark of night. For a moment, the sky is a rainbow offering a light show for those open to wonder. Each day wonder is available to behold, if only for a moment.

January 20

AN AQUARIUS GATHERS KNOWLEDGE like a jug gathers water from a well. They think and ponder questions and life lessons. Their knowledge runs deep. Ethereal and brainy at the same time, our fellow Aquarians have their heads in the clouds and feet on the ground. Seek them out for advice and they will pour it forth, but only when asked. Appreciate the intelligent and insightful Aquarius in your life.

January 21

YOUR LIFE EXPERIENCES HAVE PROVIDED you with a wealth of knowledge. You integrate experiences and knowledge well. Even when things didn't work out, there was a lesson within the falling apart. You see this and embrace it. The way we integrate life's lessons determines whether wisdom or resentment takes root. Allow time to process what's happened. Look for the wisdom available in each win, misstep, loss, and joy. Wise people are constantly learning. You hold the wealth of all this knowledge.

January 22

PLANES CIRCLE AN AIRPORT waiting to land. As they are redirected away from their original course, they create a holding pattern waiting for their signal to touch down. At times life can feel this way as we wait for answers to arrive. During these times, we can't push for the answers or do anything to hurry them along. These times are a call for patience. Eventually the answers will arrive like a plane leaving a holding pattern in the sky.

———

January 23

EXPECTATIONS CREATE A LOSS of connection to self and others. When we can accept that people operate from their own level of understanding, we can release the tight hold on how we believe things need to be. Clinging to an expectation creates a barrier that love must fight to get through. Release your grip from what your mind believes should be happening. Offer acceptance to what is. There is peace available when we let go of the ideals we cling to.

January 24

THE URGE TO BE PERFECT consumes us like a wildfire.
The smallest spark of perfection, like the compulsion to
fix something, can ignite a torrid swirl of emotions within.
Doubt, fear, and judgment are kindling to this inner turmoil.
Mindfulness can quell the flames with compassion and
love. See the struggle occurring in your mind and breathe.
Everything will be okay. Your mind was triggered and it
reacted. Keep breathing until you find yourself calming
down. Use the breath to blow out fires of perfection within.

———

January 25

DURING A STORM, WIND SHOWS its might. What was
once calm is stirred up into chaos. This powerful force
moves even the mightiest of oaks. No matter how steady
things may seem, there will always be something that can
challenge their strength. If we embrace this truth, we can learn
to be flexible during trials and bend instead of break. Release
rigidity, embrace flexibility. When a storm blows through your
life, you can remain firmly planted while bending and learning.

January 26

OUR THOUGHTS ARE ROOTED in our beliefs. What we believe to be true directs where our thoughts can wander. Growth requires that we challenge ourselves and question what we think to be true. Staying open and curious relieves the rigidity of a closed mind. What if something else is true? What if something else is meant to be? By releasing our grasp on long-held beliefs that hold us back, we can surrender into the magic of the unknown.

January 27

THE WANING OF LIGHT at day's end is only temporary. When the sun greets the horizon, the sky illuminates with an atmospheric rainbow for a brief moment. The light is the same, but the perspective is different. One day ends as another begins on the opposite hemisphere. The sun is always giving light. Seeing things from a different angle can help illuminate opportunities for healing and growth. Allowing perspectives to shift can open minds and hearts to deeper truths.

January 28

LOVE IS THE RAIN that waters barren lands. What seems hopeless can be revived with care and attention. Sorrows leave our hearts fallow, in need of healing. In time the sprouts of joy can break through. Taking time to find and recognize glimpses of love reminds us that joy and grief can occur simultaneously. Life is full of contrasts and sometimes holds opposing emotions at the same time. Allow the healing waters of love to permeate your grieving heart. Hope will take root in time.

———

January 29

THE JOURNEY TO WHOLENESS weaves one through peaks and valleys of relationship and connection. Learning to love yourself will reveal patterns and habits that may need to be surrendered in order to fully embrace your true self. This is a brave act of love because it requires letting go. Releasing what was once familiar happens with time and compassion. Give yourself grace as you embark on this journey. Love takes time.

January 30

BIRDS HOVERING OVER THE OCEAN is a good sign that a whale is nearby. Sunset is a magical hour where onlookers can spot the tails and spouts of these enormous creatures as they feed below. The most patient observer will be rewarded with these sights as whales take time to surface. Being in tune to how nature collides can welcome surprises to the most patient at the end of the day. Stillness and attention reap rewards and fill our souls with gratitude.

———

January 31

AS WE RECEIVE GOODNESS AND JOY in life, it's important to offer gratitude. Recognizing the abundance in life helps us quell our thoughts of unworthiness and scarcity. We live in a vast universe and are connected to all living beings. It's amazing how much energy surrounds us. As the day comes to an end, recognize a few things that made the day lovely. Feel it in your heart. Breathe in the joy. There are many things to be grateful for.

February 1

END YOUR DAY BY REPEATING these affirmations to yourself: *I am grateful for the lessons in my life. I honor the path I have been on and the perspectives I have gained. I offer gratitude to my past self for getting me through each obstacle. I am strong, resilient, and brave. Life is not always easy, and I am able to offer empathy and compassion to others. These lessons offer deeper respect for the joy-filled moments in my life. I honor this journey toward wisdom.*

February 2

BE TENDER WITH YOUR HEART when someone you love leaves. Losing communication and connection leaves a wound where the relationship once thrived. This grief has its own distinct pain with the possibility of seeing them again. The urge to reach out can be strong, but it doesn't help the healing process. Honor the next relationship and your heart by taking time to mend. Surround yourself with loved ones and find time for stillness. Loneliness can turn into the restorative joy of solitude.

February 3

WHEN A TREE IS HURT, IT CREATES a protective layer called "wound wood." These wounds are not uncommon, and the tree intuitively knows how to heal itself. Consider the intelligence of the tree. We also have this universal intelligence within us, which allows us to heal, soothe, and recover from hurts. These places of healing are scars that tell stories of resilience. If you are currently in a healing season, find stillness to allow your intuition to speak to and mend your body.

February 4

DETERMINATION IS LIKE AN EMBER left over after fire's destruction. Think of a time when something you desired didn't happen. Recall what took place instead of that expectation. We don't always understand why things don't work out. Sometimes understanding occurs after the fires of disappointment have burned. However, there is hope in the waiting because no matter what happens, something *is* happening. In time answers will come, and the ember of determination will spark into something beautiful.

February 5

A BIRD SOARS HIGH, drifting on air, allowing the current to help it travel. Migration is part of the bird's generational intuition. Deep within, birds know the routes that need to be taken each year. Instincts drive and help us. There are times when we ignore our intuition, and it can feel confusing. These are often unfocused or busy times. Just as a bird needs to do nothing but follow instinct to soar, we too can find answers in stillness.

———

February 6

ANGER IS AN ALL-CONSUMING EMOTION. It can burn through a relationship and leave damage in its wake. Anger is also a messenger, alerting us to boundaries that have been crossed. When the throes of anger well up, pay attention to the message they're delivering. Notice where you're feeling sensations in your body. Our bodies often know before our minds do. The more we are in tune to our body's messages, the better we can respond.

February 7

IN THE MIDST OF SURRENDER, peace can be found. Holding on to something tightly creates resistance. The yearning for what's not meant to be drives our hearts and minds toward restlessness. Holding on creates mental loops of what-ifs and obsession. And yet, peace is available on the other side of letting go. If you are holding on to something that isn't working out, slowly release your grip on it. In time what is meant to happen will have space to occur.

———

February 8

GOLDEN HOUR OCCURS right before sunset and washes everything in an amber hue. This hour contains the final moments of the sun's warmth. The end of the day is a beautiful time. This is a reminder that endings don't necessarily mean things are hopeless. There is value in the opening that closure brings. Endings can welcome something wonderful and feel as warm as the golden light at day's end. Sometimes the void is exactly where we need to be.

February 9

WHEN WE FEEL A HEADACHE or stress in our neck, it can be an invitation to notice where there is an imbalance in our lives. Stress can cause tension in our head and neck area as we clench our jaws and scrunch our shoulders. Tension is an invitation to soften. Use this message to pause and scan your mind and body for the root of the imbalance. Take your time and breathe through the discomfort. Release the urge to control and let go.

February 10

YOUR ENERGY IS SACRED. Our resources are not infinite, so it's important to protect your energy by becoming aware of the things that drain you. Notice how you feel after interactions. If you leave a place or someone feeling drained, limit your time in that environment. If certain people bring you joy and energize you, find time to surround yourself with those people. Move toward the things that are life-giving and that restore your energy.

February 11

COMMUNICATION CREATES CONNECTION. Not everyone deserves to hear your story. Find those who listen and offer true understanding. When we speak from the heart with vulnerability and truth, we allow others in. In time the practice of communicating reaps trust. It's a gift and an honor when someone shares their story with us. This trust is where respect takes root. Listen well and speak openly to strengthen the bonds of friendship and love. Little by little our relationships bloom from communication.

———

February 12

LOVE SHOWS UP WHEN WE LOOK for it and when it's least expected. The evidence of love is in the tears we cry because we loved, the laughter that returns after sorrow, and the growth in nature after a harsh winter. There are so many ways to see love's promises. It may not feel easy to search for these loving clues. Give yourself time. Seeing how life cycles through is a reminder that sorrows and joys live side by side.

February 13

THE SOLAR SYSTEM HOLDS many reminders to pause and be thankful. Seeing shooting stars, admiring the moon's cycles, and the colors of the sun rising and setting are opportunities to give thanks. Each moment of marvel reminds us that we are part of an infinite universe and connected to the flow of life. The next time you look up at the sky, remember that you contribute to the interconnectedness of the universe. Then pause and breathe in gratitude.

February 14

NO MATTER WHAT YOUR RELATIONSHIP status is, take some time to celebrate the things you love about yourself and others. If you want a partner, take some time to get specific and write down exactly what you want. If you're single, do something that makes you feel amazing. If you're partnered up, let them know how much they mean to you. If you're indifferent, do something nice for a stranger. We don't need chocolates and flowers to solidify that love is alive.

February 15

BRIDGES ARE BUILT to get to the other side. Some span miles carrying cars. Others are shorter to be taken on foot. It is amazing how the human mind created a way to cross over canyons and bodies of water. Our minds hold vast amounts of knowledge, allowing us to build ways through. When you are facing a hardship, remember the answers may not appear immediately. Be patient as you figure things out. You will make it to the other side.

———

February 16

PAY ATTENTION TO YOUR BODY. There are many physical cues that tell us what our bodies need and when to seek movement. Thirst reminds us that we need water, and hunger tells us that we need food. Notice when your mind is restless and take some time to meditate. It's easy to keep busy and ignore our body's needs. However, we function much better when we attend to each cue and learn to pay attention and nurture ourselves.

February 17

LEARNING TO EMBRACE THE GOODNESS in life can be difficult. Waiting for the other shoe to drop brings up feelings of unworthiness that can creep in, keeping us from accepting the joy that life has to offer. It can be intimidating when good things happen, but there is nothing you need to do to deserve joy. You are worthy of goodness and joy. Open your hands to receive all the good things that are on the horizon.

———

February 18

CLIMBING A MOUNTAIN is done step by step. The goal is the vista at the top, but there is splendor along the way. As the elevation increases, the flowers and trees begin to change. What was once a lush valley floor becomes rockier and steeper. Opening our eyes to how we change along the way gives us a perspective of gratitude for how far we've come. Appreciating the journey is as important as reaching the destination.

February 19

EMOTIONS ARE POWERFUL SIGNALS from our soul. A Pisces feels all the highs and lows of life deeply. As the waves of feelings swell within, they tune in to what others may fear to embrace. Behind their eyes are oceans of dreams, creativity, and intuition. When their hearts and minds are open, their sensitivity is a beautiful gift of empathy and love. Their depths are only accessed through trust and love. Appreciate the intuitive and empathic Pisces in your life.

————

February 20

WHEN THOUGHTS RACE, our inner guidance system is hijacked. The ability to decipher what we need amidst the overflow of worry can create confusion. Noticing when this happens is a good time to pause and breathe. Coming back to something as simple as breathing gives our mind a few moments to find equilibrium. Breathing in and out slowly activates our parasympathetic nervous system. Our inner guide is there waiting under the confusion. Eventually the racing inside our heads halts and calm returns.

February 21

IT'S EASY TO SEE THINGS in hindsight. We can replay how things could have been or the steps not taken when we later have space and time. Hindsight's perspective can be a catalyst for change and not shame. Instead of living in the could-haves and should-haves, see the potential for resilience and growth. Life is full of lessons and there is no map to tell us which paths to choose. Give yourself grace and embrace the insights of your choices.

————

February 22

EVERY PERSON IS BEAUTIFUL. It's a miracle that we were born. Think about all the factors that come into play to create life. Our parents are our teachers, whether we have a good or bad relationship with them. Our souls chose this time to be alive together. The timing of your life isn't a mistake. When times feel really hard, remember that you are supposed to be here right now. The world needs your gifts and presence.

February 23

WHEN HOPE FEELS LOST, look for evidence from the times when all was well. Remember the helping hands, the kind words, and the love that was given. Finding reminders of when things worked out helps to prove that all is not lost. These memories can help us breathe easier. These are the moments that stitch together the tattered remains of grief, creating a tapestry of hope. Hold on to these memories and know that eventually this time will only be a memory.

———

February 24

THE GAPS OF LOVE WE EXPERIENCED growing up may never be filled. There are many reasons a person grows up lacking the love and attention they crave. We look for ways to fill these gaps through other means, such as using food or relationships. These provide a temporary relief but only leave us craving more. Healing our hearts takes work. Over time we can accept the gaps and give love to ourselves. Through healing we are reminded that love is always available within.

February 25

DEEP IN THE FOREST ferns thrive in the shadows of the trees. In the shaded undergrowth the soil is damp. As the noon sun hovers overhead, its rays peak through the canopy, offering the ferns a few moments of light. The fern unfurls its leaves, reaching toward the light, anchored in shadows. When faced with a period of ambiguity, there are small glimmers of light. Even if they are momentary, reach for them and grow through the questions yet to be answered.

February 26

THINK ABOUT SOMEONE you love. Notice all the things you love about them. Can you recall their features and the sound of their voice? Place your hands over your heart and breathe in gratitude for this person. Send them love from your heart to theirs, noticing the energy you feel as you offer them love and gratitude. Now notice what you love about yourself! Offer love and gratitude for all the things that make you unique and special.

February 27

DANCING IS AN OUTWARD MANIFESTATION of joy.
When our bodies move to music, it's nearly impossible to
stay upset. Find your favorite song and move your body.
Don't worry about what you look like, just move. Let your
body take over and give your mind a break. Movement and
music can enhance our moods. This simple tool is available
and easily accessible. The only barrier is quieting inner
judgment and letting outer creativity be expressed.

———

February 28/29

TAKE A MOMENT TO REFLECT on the past month.
What are a few things that you enjoyed? What lessons did
this month offer to you? As you reflect on the month, note
the changes and celebrate the wins. A new month will
begin soon, offering its own highs and lows. Letting time
pass without celebrating or observing how we've changed
doesn't allow us to respect our accomplishments and
growth. It's important to appreciate the things that were
enjoyable and integrate the lessons learned.

March 1

EMBRACE THE WONDER of the rain and repeat these affirmations to yourself: *I am grateful for the rain and all the nourishment it provides. The sound of rain is a beautiful song that nature sings as it replenishes rivers and reservoirs. I embrace rainy days and celebrate the impact they have. I release my complaints and find gratitude for the weather. May the rain be plentiful and provide the earth with exactly what it needs. I look forward to discovering the growth the rain will provide.*

March 2

ANXIETY FEELS LIKE AN ELECTRICAL CURRENT pulsing through the body. It can hijack the mind, leaving one frozen in time. Fueled by fear, it's perpetuated by holding the breath. Anxiety is a signal to breathe deep and release the clenching that's causing us to stay frozen in space. Breathing can soothe this current from erratically pulsing, bringing us back to calm. When the throes of anxiety seize control of breathing patterns, pause to inhale deeply. Then exhale audibly. Repeat until you feel energy flowing more calmly.

March 3

PULLING WEEDS HELPS A GARDEN GROW. Roots need space to anchor the plant and help sprouts reach for the sun. When weeds are present, they take up soil and choke out the light. It takes work to remove unwanted growth, but the benefits are worthwhile. During seasons of growth, there are things and people that are like weeds. They take up space and energy and keep us from where we need to be. Release these ties and see your roots strengthen.

March 4

AIMING FOR PERFECTION is the desire to constantly achieve and improve. Letting go of these endless goals is a slow and transformative process. It's okay to say no and walk away from the urge to be perfect. Striving for the impossible opens the door to deep disappointment. Self-compassion and kindness bloom where perfection and rigidity once thrived. Learning to let go is a gift. Be kind to yourself when you feel the familiar tug of perfectionism. Breathe deep and let it be.

March 5

SOME FLOWERS CLOSE THEIR BLOOMS after the sun sets. In the morning, they unfurl to greet the sun, their colors as radiant as before. This daily closure is a rhythm timed with the sun. Going inward preserves energy and protects the flower from nighttime pests. We too can replenish our energy by going inward. In repose our bodies heal and filter what we don't need. Allow the sunset to be a reminder to slow down. Embrace your natural rhythms.

March 6

THE END OF A RELATIONSHIP is difficult and brings up reminders of what we settled for. Breakups also show us the things we don't like about them and ourselves. These hard truths can be painful to confront. On the other hand, they are also invitations pointing us in the direction of what we want. We can use each relationship as a guidepost on our path to love. See the lessons as keys to unlock wisdom from the experience. Healing takes time.

March 7

DEAD ENDS ARE DIFFICULT TO ACCEPT when the heart and mind want to press on. It takes time to see that what was once thriving may have reached its peak. It's important to remember that life is full of paths; some are straight and predictable, others winding and full of uncertainty, and sometimes these paths lead nowhere. Notice when a path has run out. Accept the ending. Soon you will find your way again.

March 8

A BUTTERFLY WAS ONCE A CATERPILLAR. It emerged from the disintegration of something that was once whole. From crawling to flying, a butterfly reminds us that transformation is possible and beautiful. As they flit and float from flower to flower, it seems like they live an easy life full of wonder. And yet, they know that a powerful ending created their life of ease. Sometimes the most painful endings end up being the most beautiful beginnings.

March 9

THE DREAM OF BECOMING A MOTHER is a visceral urge felt from the womb, our creative center. As the dream germinates, the desire to hold your child grows. Often a visualization of motherhood can seem so real; it is a manifestation held close to the heart. When this dream is no longer a reality, grief drapes itself heavily like a cloak. The vision disappears. You are not alone. You are still creative. Your dreams are evidence of your love.

March 10

RAIN BRINGS RELIEF to parched land after a period of drought. As the ground soaks up much-needed water, dormant plants begin to sprout. In the desert, a superbloom will occur, causing millions of wildflowers to blossom. This phenomenon can even be seen from space. Spiritual droughts can feel like scarcity and lack. Under the surface, there is a wealth of transformation waiting to sprout.Sometimes everything changes in an instant, like with a torrential downpour in the desert. Relief is on its way.

March 11

SELF-COMPASSION IS THE KIND VOICE within that tells you everything will be okay. It's easy to dismiss this voice when faced with guilt. Feeling like you've done something wrong leads to thinking up scenarios where you can right the perceived wrong. Self-compassion can swoop in and remind you that you're not alone, everyone makes mistakes. When you feel the familiar tug of guilt rising within, pause for a moment and give yourself grace. Offer yourself loving kindness.

March 12

DEEP IN THE SEA a whale can sense things that are far away. By using their senses, they are able to navigate long distances, surface safely to breathe, and communicate for survival. Through songs, clicks, and chirps, their sounds not only help them communicate, but also locate where they are in a vast ocean. These large creatures demonstrate graceful intelligence. When things in life feel too big, lean on your senses and community to navigate the depths.

March 13

RELATIONSHIPS CAN BE SOURCES OF LOVE and contentment. Think of someone that you are grateful for. See them in your mind's eye and smile. Take a moment to list the reasons why this person brings joy into your life. Write down a memory with them, detailing your experience. As you remember, notice how you feel. Write them a thank-you note for their presence in your life. When we give thanks, hearts open and relationships deepen.

March 14

IMAGINE THAT YOU'RE LYING ON the forest floor.
Allow the earth to support you as you surrender to rest.
Sink deeper into relaxation as you breathe. Feel your body
relax from your head to your toes. Let Mother Nature's
energy envelop and hold you. Whatever is troubling you
is no longer important. In this moment, prioritize surrender.
Allow answers to come and stress to melt away as you
continue to be held by this loving, healing energy of
the earth.

March 15

A SEED REQUIRES SOFTENING in order to become a
plant. Deep below the surface, water and soil permeate the
seed's coating. As the seed germinates, roots and a sprout
form. Patience, care, and time are required before the plant
bears fruit. There are many steps for a plant to become
mature, and yet, the fruit is enjoyed for a short while. When
waiting for things to take place, celebrate each step with
gratitude. The process is greater than the result.

March 16

WHEN DIFFICULTIES ARISE, they can steal our focus from everything else. Notice if the difficulty is because something needs to change or if you're being redirected. It's easy to keep trying instead of letting go, especially if it's comfortable. If you've tried several things and it still doesn't seem to be working, consider moving on to make room for what's meant to be. Redirecting our energy can help us gain perspective. We can tap into our inner guidance, and in time, the answers will be revealed.

———

March 17

MEMORIES ARE BEAUTIFUL REMINDERS of what once was. Sometimes recalling the past brings nostalgia; other times sorrow can occur. When the flood of emotion comes, spend a moment thinking about what the memory means to you. If it's joyful, offer gratitude for the delight it brought to your life. If it's sad, allow your sorrow to run its course and reflect on how your heart has mended, and sit still as the feeling passes through you.

March 18

AMBIGUOUS GRIEF LINGERS. Being unable to have closure or say goodbye weighs heavy on a heart that's searching for meaning. Don't rush the healing process. Take all the time you need to heal and find a way to embrace this ambiguity. The grief is proof that your heart had the capacity to love something not fully formed. When love is just sprouting, having it end abruptly causes confusion. There may never be answers, but the capacity to love again is possible.

March 19

THE EQUINOX IS A TIME when there is almost an equal amount of sunlight as there is night. It reminds us to honor the light of the sun. It's also a reminder that sunsets are never the same. They change depending on the time of year, the clouds in the sky, and what's floating in the atmosphere. Each evening, there is a chance to view a never-before-seen show, a limited viewing. That is how incredible our planet is.

March 20

ON A CLIFF, A RAM CLIMBS and grazes alone. He's confident in his ability to traverse difficult terrain. If he encounters a foe, he stands his ground and protects himself. He is strong, willful, and powerful. Like a ram, our Aries friends show up in their magnificence and know what they want. They go for things others may be too afraid to reach for. They show how bravery and confidence can help us achieve dreams. Appreciate the bold and confident Aries in your life.

March 21

DO YOU KNOW WHAT YOU WANT? When was the last time you identified the desires of your heart? It takes bravery to admit and declare what we want. But first, our desires need to be identified. Spend some time discovering who you are and what would bring joy and fulfillment to your life. Be bold in your discoveries. Go on a soulful treasure hunt. Ask yourself deep questions. Allow the determination to live soulfully to lead you toward fulfillment.

March 22

A GARDENER PLANTS several seeds when starting her garden. Not all will take root and become plants. Seeds are like dreams; many are needed for the success of a garden. Just because a dream doesn't come true doesn't mean something good isn't on its way to you. Sometimes our dreams are merely seeds that aren't meant to thrive. They may be clues into what we truly want. Keep planting seeds and allow your dreams to flow through you. Things will eventually make sense.

———

March 23

A HEART FULL OF COMPASSION is able to see and understand others on a deeper level. Turning inward and offering compassion to ourselves helps us understand ourselves even better. Choose to be kind and ask questions when you don't understand. Listen with an open mind. Everyone experiences life differently. Compassion will help offer insights. Love blossoms when compassion is present. Imagine the love you can offer yourself and others when you show up with tenderness.

March 24

IN A FURY OF DOING, it's easy to feel like your efforts aren't enough. When we strive to excel, achieve, and do the best, we forget to notice the tiny moments that enrich our lives. Pausing helps us to appreciate the beauty that is all around in those tiny moments. It's okay to take breaks in the midst of doing. You are enough no matter what you achieve. You deserve to take breaks and enjoy all that surrounds you. You are worthy of pausing.

March 25

A HURRICANE IS A POWERFUL FORCE, bidding the seas and winds to comply. Nature's fury swells out at sea, thrashing onto land, ruining anything in its path. After such a powerful storm blows through, it takes a long time to rebuild. Anger can feel like the fury of a hurricane in a relationship. If left unchecked, it can rip through hearts, leaving hurt and confusion in its wake. Rebuilding takes work. Ask for forgiveness when your anger causes ruin.

March 26

LIFE IS FULL OF LOVELY SURPRISES. Wildflowers bloom in a yard that seemed barren. A bird's nest hiding bright teal eggs can be found while looking at a tree. A mountain goat can appear around the bend during a long hike. Falling in love can happen when least expected. Amid life's difficulties, there are also amazing things that invite enchantment into our souls. When these surprises happen, notice the swell of excitement. Allow yourself to be inspired by life.

———

March 27

A GENTLE ANSWER CURES a bad reaction. It's easier to snap and react from the gut when upset. Taking time to calm down and respond from the heart takes strength and patience. Choose kindness when you feel the waters of anger beginning to boil. Breathe deeply, allowing your heart and mind to gently calm down. Choose to respond instead of reacting. Communication and understanding takes work. Choosing gentleness when nearing a boiling point can help soothe and restore relationships.

March 28

HOPE RISES WHEN THERE IS SOMETHING to look forward to. Can you recall a time when you were filled with the excitement of long-awaited plans? Hope thrives in the belief of things to come. Plans launch us into the future where possibilities arise. When we are ready to move forward with something, we see with expectant eyes. The anticipation sparks joy. Dreams become sweeter. Allow enthusiasm to rise. Hope is alive if we seek it.

———

March 29

WHEN THE DAY IS DONE, take time to reflect on the goodness that occurred and challenges that were overcome. Each day is a treasure chest of lessons and joys. You are not the same person from yesterday, and tomorrow will create more change. Each day offers more perspective. Since you will never have this moment or day again, reflect on the joy and embrace the lessons. You are becoming more and more yourself each day.

March 30

SURROUND YOURSELF WITH PEOPLE who love and support you, especially when things don't work out. Having a support system is a gift. It's human nature to want to try to help and find a solution, but often all that is needed is presence and the knowledge that someone is there to support. When you find the gems that can do that, hold on with love and appreciation.

March 31

THE RAIN REPLENISHES THE EARTH, providing water that is vital for growth. Rain renews, creating a supple environment for seeds to germinate and roots to expand in. Just as rain is essential for growth, water is important for us as well. Each day we have the opportunity to take care of ourselves by simply drinking enough water. This act of self-care is vital for our health and well-being. Take time to care for yourself today and stay hydrated.

April 1

AS YOU START THIS NEW MONTH, repeat these affirmations to yourself: *I am grateful for the beauty of changing seasons and the natural flow of life. I honor the time it takes for things to grow and look forward to seeing what takes root. As I continue to let go of things that no longer serve me, I embrace the lessons surrendering has provided. Nothing is permanent and I recognize that this new season is here for a short while. May I celebrate growth and be open to all possibilities.*

April 2

EVERY ONCE IN A WHILE, when the conditions are right, the sun sets between the high-rises in a city. As the sun peeks between the buildings, the street becomes ablaze in its glow. Revelers gather to watch this modern phenomenon, and for a brief moment, the city unites. It's a beautiful sight to behold—a group of people watching the sun put on a show. For a moment, the sun shines on collective awe, serving as evidence that we are all connected.

April 3

A PINE CONE HOLDS AN INTRICATE PATTERN of
scales, protecting the seeds of future trees. Rose petals
spiral surrounding the stigma. A nautilus's shell protects
its vulnerable body. Nature's designs are intelligent and
intricate. When we have an idea to create, it takes time
to share or even begin to work on it. Eventually what's
meant to take form will break through. Allow your protection
around your creation to soften in time. Masterpieces take
time to emerge.

April 4

A GARDEN BLOOMS IN ITS OWN TIME. One tree may be
full of blossoms, and another may be just beginning to bud.
Eventually both trees will bear fruit. Flower beds burst with
colors, then, in time, they are cut back. Blooming takes time.
It's easy to wonder when our moment will come to bloom.
We often measure ourselves online, with strangers, and with
our loved ones. Paths aren't linear. Trust the timing of your
life. Eventually everything will unfold like a beautiful blossom.

April 5

EVERYONE HAS A STORY TO TELL. Taking time to tell your story is an act of bravery. Taking time to listen to others' stories is an act of kindness. Even if we don't feel a personal connection to the story, we can offer respect by tuning in without distraction to hear what they have to say. There may be a lesson within the story or a connection point that has been undiscovered. Listening respects the storyteller. Telling honors the story.

———

April 6

OUR PAIN CAN BE OUR GREATEST TEACHER. Eventually the shock and hurt subside. These experiences give us time to integrate lessons learned and contemplate how to live in the outcome of what occurred. We gain perspective and eventually hope can return. Consider that a pearl is formed by a grain of sand that was once an irritant. Our healing is a testament of resilience. From this healed place, you can help others. Over time the pain becomes a pearl of wisdom.

April 7

BATS EMERGE FROM UNDERNEATH a bridge as the sun sets on the horizon. Sunset is like their alarm clock, awakening them to take flight. They arise at the perfect time to feed on insects that swirl in the golden sky. It's a phenomenon that has people flocking to Austin, Texas, to see. Just as the moon pulls the tides, the sunset is a time when several animals become active. Notice what your needs are throughout the day. Honor your inner clock.

April 8

CLOUDS DISSIPATE ACROSS THE SKY. Their colors and sizes vary, and they all eventually pass. Their moisture evaporates or precipitates, reminding us that nothing is permanent. Whether you're having a good or bad day, remember that this is just a moment in time. Be present and notice how you're feeling. If everything feels great, practice gratitude, feeling the joy that this moment provides. If you're feeling low, write it out and process how you feel. Tomorrow is full of possibilities.

April 9

WAITING IS HARD TO DO. It's even harder to trust unseen forces, especially when fear rears its head. The need to control stems from a lack of trust. This is a place for growth. Imagine all the things that needed to happen for you to be here right now. The fact that you were born is a miracle and nothing you did made it happen. This is the universe at work. There is wisdom to be found in the waiting.

April 10

OPPORTUNITIES COME AND GO. The universe is full of abundance. If you are feeling that there isn't enough, just look at nature's examples: rain after a drought, wildflowers bursting with color after a cold winter, blossoms becoming delicious fruit, and endless grains of sand! Abundance is everywhere. Next time you feel that there isn't enough, take a moment to notice that abundance is all around you. Offer gratitude and trust that your next opportunity is on its way.

April 11

ASKING FOR WHAT YOU NEED can be challenging. If
we don't voice our needs and request help when needed,
resentment has room to grow. No one can read our minds, so
communication is key. When you feel the familiar rumblings of
discontent surfacing, pause and ask yourself what you need.
Don't allow these early rumbles to become an earthquake in
your soul. Resentments grow like fault lines, cracking when
least expected. Communicate openly to release tension.

April 12

TRUE APPRECIATION FEELS LIKE LOVE. When gratitude
is shown without explanation, the receiver can revel in
the extension of kindness. To receive gratitude without
justification is a gift to the giver. Learning to give and
receive appreciation is an act of worthiness. If someone
goes out of their way to do something kind, offer gratitude
from your heart. Consider the time they took to think of
you and honor their effort. When someone offers gratitude,
receive it with love.

April 13

WE CAN BE OUR OWN HARSHEST CRITIC. The judgments we have toward others often mirror what we are thinking inwardly about ourselves. Self-judgment is complicated to break free from. Self-compassion is an invitation to be kind and loving. When the impulse of judgment begins to surface, pause and think of something kind to say or think. If you can't think of anything, simply breathe and allow the impulse to judge to pass.

April 14

GRACE IS MORE IMPORTANT than doing. Sometimes we need to give ourselves a break, especially when we are doing it to earn favor. It's hard to give grace when acknowledgment and achievement are the main drivers in life. But they create a never-ending feedback loop, leaving the achiever on high alert. Be kind to your nervous system and stop the loop. Break the cycle of constant achievement by giving yourself grace and time for serenity.

April 15

BOREDOM CAN OCCUR when waiting for things to happen. The urge to reach for a phone or another numbing device is a reflex to soothe the discomfort. This period of waiting can be a rich time of inner growth. When the schedule is clear, there is time to be still. In stillness answers arrive, nervous systems find balance, and we learn to appreciate our own company. Resist the urge to distract. Welcome the enriching challenge of being still.

April 16

REFLECTING ON THE PAST can be beneficial because it shows how far you've come. What seemed like unanswered questions can be reviewed with the perspective of time. Think about your younger self and the desires you held close to your heart. Notice the ones that happened and the others that did not. Thank your past self for getting you this far and for all the dreaming and letting go you've done. You are exactly where you're meant to be right here, right now.

April 17

NATURE SINGS BEAUTIFUL MELODIES if we stop to listen. Different bird songs can be heard throughout the day. The tides rise and fall, offering music along soft sand and rocky jetties. Wind rustles through the leaves, swinging branches, scratching here and there. At sunset, humans sigh in awe as the sun says farewell to the day. When we tune in to the sounds around us, we can appreciate nature's songs. What melodies did you hear today?

———

April 18

WE CAN'T ALWAYS KNOW how things will work out. That's the beautiful mystery of life. We can search for clues and sometimes they lead us toward realizations. Not knowing helps us practice patience. There is joy in the journey, which fuels the excitement for the anticipated outcome. No matter where the path may lead, know that along the way, the next step will be revealed. Each step can be a destination in itself.

April 19

IGNORING SORROWS ONLY GIVES THEM POWER.
We can't stuff them away like discarded socks. Grief needs
attention to move through our hearts. It's uncomfortable to
feel it all but there is healing in the feeling. Unresolved grief
can manifest in many different ways, and also when least
expected. If you're in a grieving period, allow your sorrow
to move through you. Seek support and process what has
happened. Your feelings are proof that you love deeply.

———————

April 20

STRONG AND STEADY, a bull goes after what he wants.
He takes his time enjoying his food, slowly appreciating
everything around him. Named after a bull, the Taurus sign
reminds us to slowly enjoy life's pleasures. Our Taurus friends
are masters of luxury. They go after what they want and
take their time enjoying life's pleasures. Because they live
life to the fullest, they attract others to them easily. They are
compassionate and generous to the people they love. Offer
appreciation to the steady and patient Taurus in your life.

April 21

VIBRANCY EMANATES FROM WITHIN. When we feel good in our mind, body, and soul, we give off a light that attracts others to us. To cultivate more vibrancy, do the things that make you light up. Find the people that leave you feeling loved and energized. Say no to things that don't align with your soul. Release obligations that drain you. Follow your instincts and learn about what interests you. Share your gifts with others and don't be afraid to shine your vibrant light!

April 22

YOUR BODY IS YOUR SOUL'S PHYSICAL HOME. It's sacred and deserves love, care, and attention. Taking care of our bodies includes water, movement, sunshine, and kindness. Think of your body as a houseplant. Tend to it carefully. Speak kindly to it and water it daily. Move it into the sunshine so it can grow and open. Stretch often. Affirm your amazing existence and the miracle of having a physical home for your sacred soul.

April 23

WHISPER "I LOVE YOU" TO YOURSELF each day. This is a loving reminder that helps us on the days when it's most difficult to love. The words "I love you" hold the power to open closed-off hearts and mend the ones that are breaking. These words also affirm when everything feels on track and joyful. This sweet whisper will build a loving muscle that can help on the heavier days. Every one of us is worthy of great love.

April 24

IT TAKES TIME FOR THINGS to find balance. After a storm, the dust settles and the water calms. The same is true after going through difficulties. We need time to understand the experiences that challenge us. Growth and wisdom come from the space between the event and restoration. In this time, be patient with yourself. Your soul is making meaning and finding acceptance. Honor whatever space you are in. Eventually you will find your balance once more.

April 25

WHEN YOU FEEL THE URGE TO REACT, remember to breathe. Allow your breath to move the energy through you as you settle your nervous system. Our sympathetic nervous system is activated when we are triggered, causing the pull to react. Taking time to pause and breathe can help us calm down and respond instead of reacting. Noticing when these moments arise is the first step. Always remember to breathe. Your breath and awareness are where healing begins.

———

April 26

WHEN CHANGES OCCUR, it can feel good to do things to move the change along. Sometimes the most important thing to do though is pause. There are so many answers available when we invite stillness into our lives, especially during change. Staying busy doesn't necessarily mean making progress! To hear your intuition, get quiet and listen for the answers. This may take some time. When you feel clarity has occurred, take action. Change will happen in perfect timing.

April 27

HOME IS A PLACE TO SETTLE your soul and feel comfortable being who you are. Our homes are a nest to retreat to when the day is done or when a break is needed. Create a sanctuary in your home by placing things with care and choosing items that ground you. Clear the air by putting away clutter and opening the windows. Let the light in and breathe in gratitude for the place you call home.

———

April 28

BE OPEN TO THE LOVE available to you. Receive it with grace. If it's hard to accept the love that is being extended, check in with yourself and notice why. Sometimes past hurts can keep us from giving and receiving love. You are worthy of a great love and don't need to do anything to deserve it. See the people who extend love to you as an extension of the love you give. Open up to love and invite connection in.

April 29

LIVING WITH COMPASSION recognizes the humanity in all of us. When we see ourselves as part of a greater whole, we see that our trials are not singularly on us. Everyone experiences struggles and joys. At times it's easier to offer compassion to another, and yet, self-compassion is necessary to healing. If you're going through a difficult time, remember that you are not alone. Extend the same compassion you would to a friend and allow time to mend.

April 30

POSSIBILITIES ARE EVERYWHERE. Each day provides a new possibility to dream, do, and be. At times it may feel like there isn't anything happening and reality feels frustrating. During these times, taking things one day at a time is essential for well-being. When we worry about the things that could happen, it causes unease. Taking time to pause and reflect on the day and moments in front of you will create the possibility for a moment of calm.

May 1

GENTLY REPEAT THESE AFFIRMATIONS as you appreciate your body: *I am grateful for my body and everything it does for me. I'm grateful for my organs and all the intricate systems that are within me. My body is a divine design and it's amazing how everything works together. I'm grateful for my senses that allow me to taste amazing food, see beautiful sunsets, hear the birds chirp, smell the rain, and feel a warm embrace. I love my body and offer gratitude and awe for each part and function.*

May 2

ABUNDANCE IS AVAILABLE to us if we look below the surface. Often feelings of jealousy, discontent, and fear can keep us from seeing the goodness waiting to break through. Our minds are powerful, and if we are tuned in to negative thoughts, we will see things in a negative and scarce light. Keep searching for goodness like the variety of flowers on your walk or the colors in the sky. Dig deeper and search to see what's keeping you from finding the energetic flow of abundance. Welcome it with worthiness and gratitude.

May 3

WHAT NEEDS HEALING will bother us until we attend to it. A wound needs care and time to heal. If there is resentment in your heart, offer some compassion to the situation to begin the healing process. This may include forgiveness, reconciliation, or letting go. Resentment is a soul wound and if left unattended, it can infect the life you live. Be gentle with yourself as you take the time to recover from this place of hurt.

May 4

SUNSETS OFFER A REPRIEVE from the relentless desert heat. As the sun sets, it casts its final light on the surrounding rocks. Mountains glow in the warm light, looking ablaze. The final rays change browns to a soft, salmon pink. The day's end brings cooler temperatures and a changing of the guard. Lizards burrow while coyotes emerge. Another cycle of movement begins as the desert never sleeps. Life is in constant motion. When we take pauses, we can see how much change is occurring.

May 5

IN THE MIDST OF TRIALS, hope shows up when it's most needed. After a frosty winter, the sun warms the ground. Little plant shoots pop through the thawed soil, a symbol of hope after a long winter. At times it can feel like the waiting is extended and your patience can be tried. During prolonged times of uncertainty, notice where small signs of hope begin to appear. Even the smallest sprout can become a mighty oak.

May 6

JEALOUSY POINTS US TO SOMETHING we wish we had. It can start as a small thought and grow into an all-consuming obsession. The desires that envy fuels keep us from appreciating what's right in front of us. Remember that everyone lives a different life filled with their own struggles and joys. Jealousy is a clue and an invitation to step toward your desires and to be thankful for what you already have.

May 7

OUT IN THE OCEAN a bed of kelp bobs in the water.
As the waves rise and fall, the kelp bed is fluid, yet stays
rooted in place on the rocks below. It moves with the tides,
providing a rich environment for sea life. It may feel difficult
to stay grounded when the waves of grief rise and fall.
Finding people who feel safe to help ground you can provide
comfort and compassion during turbulent times. Connection
is a lifesaver.

May 8

SCARCITY IS AN INVITATION to pause, breathe, and
recognize the abundance in our lives. When scarcity shows
up, it can mask itself as envy, yearning, and anxiety. When
we compare ourselves to others what we lack creates a
longing and eventually it can become a fixation. However,
we are invited to look at what we do have and identify
where abundance has shown up in our lives. When we
redirect our attention to abundance, contentment can
soothe our longing hearts.

May 9

FEAR IS A MESSENGER that can hinder our growth. Fear wants to remind us of everything that could go wrong. It also alerts us when something is wrong, which can keep us frozen in place when it's time to move forward. Overcoming fear takes mindfulness and patience. Taking time to notice what our internal alert system is saying is helpful. If fear is freezing you in place, thank it for showing up and then take one step to move forward toward your goals.

May 10

SUNSETS PROVIDE AN ARRAY of colors to behold. They are a reminder of all the beautiful hues that surround us. From the sky's ever-changing color to the shades of our skin, color brings vibrancy and variety to life. Think about your favorite color and something that displays its beautiful hue. Notice how this color makes you feel. If you can, display this color in your home to inspire this feeling each day.

May 11

HOLD ON TIGHT to the people you love and who show up when you need them. We all desire to be loved in our own way. When someone loves us the way we need to be loved and not the way they do, it's a beautiful offering. Recognize the love you receive with deep gratitude. We are all different, like plants, requiring various amounts of love, attention, and care. When tended to properly, thriving and growth occurs.

May 12

WHEN THINGS FEEL LIKE THEY AREN'T WORKING out, stop trying to make things work. Surrender to the unknown. This space can be a magical place for new beginnings and understanding if stillness is welcomed. Welcome this time of uncertainty. The urge to perform tasks and do something can be a way to escape the discomfort of the unknown. Allow yourself to sink into the mystery, and allow answers to occur. Let the mystery and magic surprise and enchant you.

May 13

A MAIDEN WAITS TO BE RESCUED. It's a tale that's seeped into our narrative. No matter the work that's done to change this narrative, the legend remains. There is a part of each of us that would love to be rescued. That small self inside of us calls out. But we don't need to be rescued and can go through the threshold of growth on our own. It's here where we must encounter a change, which is often met with difficulty. Through this ordeal, we learn the power has always been within.

May 14

A HIBISCUS BLOOMS in vibrant colors. It showcases large flowers with striking centers attracting birds to its nectar. These flowers have been used in teas and other remedies for many years. They offer vibrancy to the eye and body. The way we take care of our bodies is just one part of true vibrancy. Our souls also need attention. To bloom bright, we need time in stillness to tend to our spirit. Take time to bloom by tending to the body and the soul.

May 15

WILDFIRES RIP THROUGH A FOREST, burning everything
in their path. Some are easily contained, others grow
with the help of wind and dry vegetation, leaving charred
destruction behind. Grief can consume like the flames of
a wildfire. It can seep into our hearts and souls, shutting
us down to comfort and compassion. But eventually the
burning slows down to a smolder and then ash, making way
for growth to occur once more.

———

May 16

FINDING BALANCE IS FUNDAMENTAL to our well-being.
We live in a society that honors productivity, but it's time
to look deeper into why we are so stressed out and looking
for ways to escape. If we took more time to listen to our
bodies, we'd learn how much our minds, muscles, and
nervous systems are begging for equilibrium. Notice when
and where your stability is compromised. Create boundaries
where needed and say no more often. Allow yourself to
learn how to value your needs.

May 17

TAKE A MOMENT TO RECALL a time when you felt a sense of awe. Where were you? What was happening? How did you respond? Do any sights, sounds, or smells come up as you recall this memory? Allow yourself to marinate in this feeling of gratefulness. Breathe in the peace this memory invokes. Invite this pause of wonder and remind your mind and body that they are capable of feeling this good.

May 18

IN THE EARLY EVENING, birds circle over the ocean, diving in to catch their final meals of the day. The sun has started to set below the horizon and the dolphins below act as guides for these hungry birds. It's a magnificent sight to behold with the peach-and-indigo sky. The birds are making the most out of the final moments of sunlight, seizing the day. Every sunset is an opportunity to offer gratitude for the day's beautiful moments.

May 19

WHEN OUR BODIES ARE INJURED, impatience can well up during the healing process. Being used to feeling good can add to the frustration of an injury. However, giving grace to our bodies and taking time to heal is an act of self-compassion. Our bodies are intelligent and need time, space, and sometimes medical intervention to heal. Be gentle with yourself; it's okay to slow down. Take it easy and allow healing to occur.

May 20

INVESTING IN YOURSELF CAN FEEL HARD if you've spent your life putting others before you. Although helping others is honorable, ignoring your needs leaves you drained. Take care of yourself first. When we give from an empty cup, we can forgo our wants and needs, leaving us resentful and exhausted. It's important to take good care of yourself before pouring into others. Creating healthy boundaries can protect your energy making sure there is enough to go around.

May 21

NEVER TAKING ANYTHING at face value, our Gemini friends show us the importance of truth. Their curious nature helps them question, uncover, and discern. They can see both sides and represent the power of communication between them. Communication is the key to a healthy relationship. Get curious when something feels off-balance. Look for ways to uncover the truth. Being able to see both sides and not get caught up in your own story is wise. Offer appreciation for the extraordinary Gemini in your life.

May 22

TRUTH LIBERATES WHEN ambiguity threatens trust. At times we are unsure of what we want or how to seek the answers. We can get caught up in what-ifs. It's easy to let uncertainty swirl in our heads, pulling us into various scenarios. Reaching out to a trusted mentor can help sift through the confusing thoughts and give perspective. Identify and appreciate the people you trust with your stories. When we have someone who listens and offers sound advice, we can find clarity.

May 23

SERENDIPITY SHOWS UP when least expected. Finding magical connections out of nowhere is special and affirms that good things are all around. Notice the moments when things seem to fall into place. Appreciate how they appear. Pause to allow the feeling of awe wash over you as you revel in the magical moment. There is bliss in the unexpected coincidences that show up from time to time. Serendipity is like the universe affirming its presence in our lives.

May 24

A SPIDER'S WEB IS AN INTRICATE DESIGN, inspiring creativity and dedication. Some spiders create their detailed designs every day. Webs are sources of survival as food gets trapped in their sticky spirals. The spider doesn't worry what others may think, it creates because it must. The same can be said with any creative pursuit. We are all creative and although expressed differently, when we create, we feed our souls.

May 25

IN A WORLD THAT IS THRIVING online, we can sometimes ignore the soul's needs. And one of the best ways to tap into those needs is away from our devices, in stillness. It's easy to hustle, scroll, achieve, compare, and numb uncomfortable feelings. It's hard to be still, listen for soulful cues, and heed their calls because most of the time they aren't seen or appreciated. Pause, check in, and unplug. Your nervous system will thank you for taking the time.

May 26

IT'S EASY TO GET STUCK in negative thoughts. If you feel like things aren't working out, pause the negative feed that runs through your mind. Scarcity thrives in these incessant loops. When feeling scarce, finding reminders of abundance can help us see that this negative state is temporary. Abundance is more than monetary wealth. It comes in many forms: time, energy, and love. When we look for it, we can find something good. Looking for evidence of goodness changes things.

May 27

STAINED GLASS CASTS A RAINBOW across the wall. As the sun begins to lower, the rainbow makes its way down the wall. Each color is a fragment of the window creating this lovely dance of hues. Our lives are made of fragments; some parts are broken, others are glimmering lights. If we take a step back, we see that we contain a rainbow within, a multitude of colors and shades, full of raw radiance. Embrace the fragments as they are just pieces of an entire life.

May 28

SPEND TIME DOING THINGS that tap into your purpose. It's easy to spend our days distracted and focused on things that don't fulfill. Each day is an opportunity to do something that invites in purpose. Whether it's part of a paid job, creativity, or relating to others, when you act from purpose, time flows. To find your purpose, notice the things that people often go to you for and the things where time seems to disappear. The answers are in these clues.

May 29

IT'S HARD TO MEND A RELATIONSHIP after a hurt has happened. Shutting down feels protective and insulates the heart from more hurt. It takes time to allow a closed heart to open back up. Being the first to attempt to repair the rift takes courage. If you're not ready, give yourself space to heal from the hurt. If the relationship is important and worth salvaging, try to repair it. Lower the drawbridge from the fortress surrounding your heart, and slowly welcome them back in.

———

May 30

RIGHT BEFORE A STORM, the sunset blazes red and orange across the sky. It warns of the rain and wind coming offshore. This clue from nature can help us prepare for what's to come. Paying attention to subtle shifts allows us to anticipate needs. A daily gratitude practice is one way we can prepare for the storms in life. When we can see the goodness in life, we are able to weather emotional upheavals that occur.

May 31

WHEN YOUR BODY BETRAYS your dreams, loving yourself
seems impossible. The mind can create dream scenarios
and becomes attached to these outcomes. Sometimes
these dreams and expectations aren't meant to be. It's a
heartbreaking realization to learn this truth. And yet, your body
is still amazing, and those dreams are the truth of your ability
to love and hope. The body will mend. Hope will eventually
return. The heart reopens. Life is beautiful that way.

June 1

AS YOU ACKNOWLEDGE ALL THAT YOU HAVE ENDURED, repeat these affirmations to yourself: *I am grateful for the resilience I have learned through the trials I have endured. I am brave and powerful. When life is hard, I have found ways to overcome and grow. Even when I doubted myself and the process, I was able to make it through. Each year my wisdom deepens. Resilience has helped me set boundaries where needed, glean wisdom where available, and learn to trust my intuition. I am grateful for each lesson and look back on my life with pride.*

June 2

WHEN THE DAY IS BUSY, it is easy to feel caught up in stress. There will always be something to do and energy to exert. And it's important to take time to ground yourself each day. Find a beach and watch the sunset. Stand barefoot on a lawn and feel your feet sink into the earth. Place your hand on a tree and feel its ancient, calming energy. Allow yourself to be held by nature's loving energy.

June 3

IT'S NEVER TOO LATE to forge a new path in life. Your ideas and dreams deserve exploration. There may be hints of your purpose within each idea to bring you closer to fulfillment. Not all plans will work out, but trying something new will create change within. Bravery blooms in the trying. Resilience takes root when things don't work out. Confidence shows up the more we try to get back up. Your dreams are yours for a reason.

June 4

IT CAN FEEL SATISFYING TO JUDGE because it transfers negative feelings onto others. However, judgment only perpetuates the pain that we feel within. Instead of riding the wave of temporary relief that judgment can bring to our critical minds, we can stop and recognize what's truly hurting. When we do this, we release the grip judgment has on our minds. We see the humanity of others and extend understanding. With practice, releasing judgment expands our acceptance of ourselves and those around us.

June 5

WIND MOVES ACROSS THE BAY causing ripples on the surface, disturbing what was once calm. As they move, the ripples catch sparks of light from the setting sun. The wind and water dance together as the sunset offers its warm light. What may seem like a disturbance can offer the movement needed to show off talents and beauty. Allow life to feel unsettled, like a windy bay, as you begin to share your gifts. Your creations are a beautiful offering.

June 6

LOVE LOOKS PAST THE WOUNDS of youth and broken armor of past relationships. Love reaches through the tangle of protective netting and shows up time and again. Our hearts may feel broken, but love will continue to show up. It works its way through the tangles and wounds until all that's left is an open hand to hold. Love heals and is available without looking too far because it can be found within us. Our true essence is love.

June 7

CONTROL DISGUISES ITSELF AS the need to know and help. Sometimes our desire to step in causes stress and anxiety when all the details aren't laid out. This is a warning signal from your nervous system. When you feel alerted, stop yourself from reacting with urgency and breathe. Remind yourself of your true intentions and let go of the need to know. Everything will fall into place. All you can do is show up with an open mind and hands to help.

June 8

A LETTER FOR AN OVERWHELMED MIND: *Dear Mind,*
Please be kind to my heart and body. When you feel that
familiar reaction to judge, choose to let it pass and instead
lift me up. I am choosing to change the negative pathways
that are so deeply ingrained within. I choose to replace them
with kindness, patience, and understanding. I am ready to
welcome joy and connection where cynicism and protection
once thrived. Thank you for all you do. Thank you for keeping
me safe.

June 9

A LETTER FOR A HURT HEART: *Dear Heart, I'm ready*
for you to open back up. I know life has been hurtful and
scary. It's painful when understanding and connection are
lost. And yet, I've felt and seen your enormous capacity to
love. You are so big, and it's taken a lot of work to keep you
hidden. So, I am slowly letting down my guard of the walls
that have been built to protect you. Thank you for showing
me what's important.

June 10

LIFE WOULD BE AMAZING if everything could work out at all times. It would be much easier if we never had to worry and if anxiety stayed at bay. However, resilience, courage, and empathy are just a few skills that take root from trials. When we notice how the hard times made us stronger, we can embrace our strength. If you're feeling overwhelmed, remember that underneath the weight of the stress, your strength is growing.

June 11

MAKING EXCUSES ONLY PROLONGS the healing process. It's easy to transfer the blame when things aren't going well. Complaints allow us to take a break from the work that growth requires. Sometimes a situation calls for acceptance. Other times a change is needed. If this is the case, take one small step each day to make the change. Resist the urge to complain and blame. Breathe through the discomfort. Important changes require time and effort. In time healing will occur.

June 12

LOVE IS AN ACTION of pouring into another to meet their needs and affirm their existence. Coming from a place of pure intention, love feels warm and nurturing. Notice how you are giving love. Do you feel a pull to keep score? Does love pour through you effortlessly? Giving love without expectation is one of the greatest gifts. If expectations are present, tend to your heart before pouring love into another. We are all worthy of love.

June 13

A DEAD END CAN BE A NEW BEGINNING. When we drive into a street with a dead end, we turn around. Eventually there are other streets to turn onto. We don't have to go all the way back from where we began. Embrace the redirection. This may be the direction toward the answers you've been seeking. Explore other roads and enjoy the views. Life is an adventure and a little bit of bravery can propel us into paths we didn't even realize existed.

June 14

TEARS CAN FALL ENDLESSLY when sorrow visits. This flood of emotion can feel like you're drowning in sorrow. Look for the lifeboats that come your way in the sweet memories that are remembered, the quiet stillness of a friend nearby, a hug that comforts and soothes. Even if these are momentary, each lifeboat offers a breath of relief from the vast ocean of sorrow to cross. These small acts will help keep us afloat through the waters of grief.

June 15

THE ALLURE OF TRAVEL TAKES US to dreamy landscapes and awe-inspiring places. Travel can fill the senses and bring appreciation for the world we live in. Time away can also elicit a deeper appreciation for home. Travel is amazing, but not always comfortable. Upon return, contentment for the life that you've created blooms. It's lovely to get away and even better to come home to the comfort and environment that you created.

June 16

A DEER LIES DOWN IN A MEADOW to sleep. It is calm
and feels safe. There are times when it is on high alert,
looking out for predators. Its heart races and adrenaline
courses through its veins. The reprieve of safety allows its
nervous system to calm down. When it must get back up,
its instincts can keep it alert and safe. Learn from the deer
and take time each day to reset your nervous system to
find calm.

June 17

THE EXPECTATIONS OF OTHERS cause disappointment
and heartache. We can't control the actions or feelings
of others. Letting go of what we expect from them is the
gateway to healing relationships. Practicing compassion
and allowing yourself to let go of an ideal that won't happen
will pave a more loving path ahead. When we see people
for who they are and not what we expect, we can offer
acceptance. Release your grasp on the ideal and open your
heart to what is.

June 18

YOU ARE WORTHY OF GOODNESS and love. When good things come into your life, accept them with joy and gratitude. It's easy to allow self-sabotage to kick in and wait for the other shoe to drop. However, this is only fear showing up to protect you from the possibility of disappointment. The next time joy shows up, notice when fear starts to creep in and pause. Breathe and tell yourself that everything will be okay and that you are worthy.

———

June 19

GRIEF DOESN'T GO AWAY with time. We grow around our grief just as a river flows around a boulder. The water may wear down the rock but its presence persists. What may look like an impediment is only a detour in the great river of life. Dreams return unexpectedly. One day the perspective of grief will make the dreams feel more magical. When grief enters your life, feel through it and know that the ability to dream will eventually flow once again.

June 20

THE SUMMER SOLSTICE WELCOMES the longest day of the year. This is a time for celebration and excitement for the season ahead. With more sunlight available, fruit is able to ripen and warmer temperatures welcome activity. Summer is a time of promise and dreaming. Choose a way to welcome this season with joy. Find ways to incorporate play and relaxation, especially if you have a busy schedule. Soak up the extra sunlight and offer gratitude for the ripening that's occurring.

June 21

A CRAB IS RESOURCEFUL and carries its home on its back. It protects its vulnerability, coming out only when needed and it feels safe. It is sensitive to the ebbs and flows of the tides. Our fellow Cancers are some of the most nurturing and compassionate people. They are intuitive and can feel how others are feeling, sometimes before the other person realizes how they feel. They know how to nurture others or be still when needed. Appreciate the nurturing and loving Cancer in your life.

June 22

YOU ARE THE ENERGY THAT NURTURES and gives. Homes are created with your creativity and passion. You feel the depths that others may fear to visit because you know that healing comes through feeling. Mother energy comes from those who offer parts of themselves through love and compassion. Mother energy is available to all and can be given by all. When we harness the parts of ourselves that are open to nourishing others through love, we've tapped into our inner well.

June 23

A RAINBOW IS A PRISM OF LIGHT reflecting off of water. It's amazing to see every color in the spectrum arching across the sky. It's a reminder that eventually storms pass and that meaning can be found through every trial. If you're going through one of life's storms, look for glimpses of hope. They can be found in the simplest places. Find something lovely to capture in your mind's eye and offer gratitude for the reminder of hope to come.

June 24

THE SWEET BERRIES OF SUMMER are ready to be enjoyed after months ripening on the vine. If picked too early, they are bitter and tart. If picked too late, they are mushy and sour. Waiting for ripening takes patience and awareness. When you're in a period of waiting, let go of control and stay aware enough to know when to act. Everything will happen when the time is right. Be patient; you are ripening!

June 25

WHEN MOTHER EARTH SPEAKS, listen. As the planet continues to warm up we are experiencing floods, fires, storms, and changing gulf streams. Rising temperatures cause a ripple effect of discomfort on land and in the sea. Each of us can create a wave of change by choosing to pay attention and changing habits. Future generations are counting on us to secure a beautiful future. When the earth offers signals, choose to listen to Mother Earth's call.

June 26

NEW BEGINNINGS ARE INSPIRING times and filled with joy. Looking forward from a place of anticipation is exciting. When our dreams are just seeds, it may seem like a long time before they occur. Sometimes we are redirected to something greater than our dream. The place between the dream and reality is filled with lessons that deepen gratitude with a new beginning. All the time dreaming and planning will feel worth it when things fall into place.

June 27

OUR STRENGTHS ARE MEANT TO BE USED and celebrated. When the work you do doesn't utilize your strengths, look for ways to incorporate them. We shine our brightest when we share our talents with the world. Each of us offers something unique. If you're unsure what your strengths are, ask people close to you what they believe you're good at. Notice what others come to you for. These answers hold the clues to where your strengths lie.

June 28

GOOD FRIENDS MAKE LIFE BEAUTIFUL and bearable. Having people in your life that see you and accept you for who you are takes vulnerability and trust. Think about someone who has shown up when you needed them, helped you grow as a person, and offers understanding. Notice how you feel as you remember their kindness and love. Make some time to let them know how much you appreciate them.

June 29

WHEN WE LIVE IN A STATE OF EXPECTING something from others, we set ourselves up for frustration. No matter how many times we intend to release expectations, there will be an opportunity to release again. We all want things the way we want them and when we want them. But, we can't control others. When expectations show up and frustration threatens your joy, pause and let go once again. This practice is a reminder that growth is always available.

June 30

TEACHERS AND MENTORS are one of life's greatest treasures. Having someone take the time to offer guidance and nurturing is empowering. When someone chooses to invest their time in our growth, offer appreciation. We learn through their examples, wisdom, and resilience. Think of someone who was a teacher or mentor to you. Take some time to thank them for the impact they had on your life and the lessons you learned through them. Your words will be a gift to them.

July 1

AS YOU END YOUR DAY, repeat these affirmations to yourself: *I am grateful for the sun's bright light and warm rays. I love how the flowers reach toward the light in the noonday sun. I love how my skin feels when emerging from the shade and into the sun. I'm grateful that the sun rises and sets in colorful radiance casting a rose-gold glow in its path. I love that the sunrise excites me for a new day and the sunset reminds me of the goodness that occurred.*

July 2

THERE ARE TIMES WHEN IT TAKES LONGER than expected to get over something. We can hold on to memories, searching for answers or clues to why things happened. It's okay to take time to process. Healing comes through the processing. Consider a summer sunset and the gravid pause the sun takes before dipping below the horizon. The extra time is perfect for reflection. The pace of your healing isn't a race. You are right on time.

July 3

WHEN OUR THOUGHTS ARE RACING, our inner guidance system is hijacked. Anxiety and fear sweep in, making it feel like peace is unattainable. When our inner compass spins it fails to find our true north. Notice the spinning and take a breath. This pause is the first step to allowing our minds to find equilibrium. Recognize the thoughts that are racing. Stop the spinning, decelerate the race, ground yourself by counting your breaths. Eventually your inner compass will recalibrate and find its north.

July 4

WHEN DIFFICULT THINGS HAPPEN, there can be a tendency to downplay grief by saying, "Well, I guess it's not as bad as…" There is no need to apologize for the way you feel. Honor your grief as it doesn't measure itself based on the severity of the event. Grief is hard no matter the reason for the loss. Although it's a heavy subject, it's through sharing these stories that resilience and hope shine through.

July 5

THE SUN MUST SET so a firefly can shine. As the night becomes darker, fireflies are easier to spot. Their quick and neon flickers can be seen fluttering around. It's a magical sight to behold on a summer night. Sometimes we don't see the purpose behind an ending. We hold on to what is familiar, and yet, in the darkness, answers can be revealed. Know that in the uncertainty, flickers of clarity, like the light of a firefly, will appear.

July 6

A MENTOR CAN HELP US FIND OUR WAY when all seems lost. It's easy to get in our heads, stuck in the particulars. It can feel like a void with no end or answers in sight. Having someone you trust to walk beside you can shed light where once there seemed to be nothing. They can guide you past the places where your mind gets stuck and help you find your way to the light at the end of the tunnel.

July 7

ROSES OFFER A SWEET AROMA for those willing to pause and smell them. Roses also have the highest vibrational frequency in their scent, which has also been attributed to feelings of love. A short moment of mindfulness can welcome these vibrations into your day. Infuse love and wonder by stopping to notice their scent and intricate spiral of their petals. Allow this moment of mindfulness to calm your mind and activate your heart toward love.

July 8

ONCE A TORNADO STARTS SPINNING, it takes time and energy to disperse. In the aftermath, debris is left in its tracks. Negative thoughts rip through our minds like a tornado, leaving thought debris in our pathways to remind us that things aren't okay. Fear causes scarcity and worry to swirl in our minds. There is work that can be done to clean up this debris. Gratitude can change our minds and help us replace scarce thoughts with ones of being and having enough.

July 9

HELPING OTHERS BRINGS JOY to the giver and receiver. It brings us out of our minds, creates connection, and extends kindness. There are so many people who need help and there are wonderful organizations doing good in the world. Finding ways to exchange energy in a positive way can also give perspective to life. Seeing things from another's point of view can help us gain understanding of things that are outside of us. Create ripples of loving kindness by choosing to help.

July 10

ENDLESS NEWSFEEDS FILL OUR MINDS with what has and can possibly go wrong. Stories of heartache and terror often make the front page. We often have to open the paper to find the stories of inspiration. When we look past the surface, there is a depth of wonder to behold. Opening is where the beautiful unexpected is uncovered. Open your eyes, heart, and mind to what's around you. Be open to seeing, feeling, and thinking differently. Allow inspiration to find and amaze you.

July 11

THE DRIVE TO ACCOMPLISH great things is honorable but can also keep us from living life fully. When we calibrate our minds toward achieving goals and bucket lists, we can miss the simple joys of each day. Finding balance in our pursuit of greatness will keep us grounded and present. Look for the simple pleasures in each day. Cherish the moments as they pass. See the goodness in yourself regardless of what you accomplish. Celebrate just being you.

July 12

ENCOURAGE THOSE WHO NEED SUPPORT. If someone is struggling, offer them words of encouragement or an ear to listen. Be there for them. Sometimes just knowing that someone is in our corner is enough to brighten a difficult situation. Often we don't need solutions, just someone to stand beside us and listen. Connection is more powerful than advice. Show up in love and know that your presence can relieve feelings of loneliness and disconnection.

July 13

HOPE IS A FLAME THAT BURNS in the midst of trials. When all seems lost, our ability to hold on to hope helps us move forward. If it feels like you're hanging on by a thread, look to the places where hope is still alive. Offer gratitude for what is working and release everything else. When things don't work out, find hope in what's to come. Even a spark can grow into a raging fire with enough attention and care.

July 14

THE MORE WE LEARN about space, the more we see how little we know. Knowledge can add to bewilderment. We are part of an infinite universe, and the more it's explored, the more awe-inspiring it becomes. The births of stars, galaxies, and supernovas are being photographed like never before. Recognize with astonishment that your soul decided consciousness for this moment in time. Breathe in gratitude for the experience of being alive on this little planet in the vastness of the universe.

July 15

CONSIDER THE PROCESS a caterpillar undergoes in
a cocoon. Deep inside, there is a void, an unknowing
of what's to come. The void is the liminal space before
transformation. It's the place where meditation, prayer,
and silence are needed. It's a sacred space to allow life to
unfold. Eventually the caterpillar's metamorphosis helps
to push it out of the cocoon, spread its wings, and fly as
a butterfly. The liminal space is where stillness helps us
uncover and integrate our next stage.

July 16

WHEN WE ARE FRUSTRATED, it's easy to take it out
on the person closest to us. They are who we are most
intimate with and feel safe to show all sides of ourselves
to. Even though they are there and accept us, they deserve
consideration when we are upset. By simply stating that you
are frustrated and need a space to process, their urge to fix
or defend can ease. From this space, they can give you a
place to vent. Offer them appreciation for their time and for
being a safe place in your life.

July 17

TRAVELING OPENS OUR EYES to the unfamiliar. Whether it's to a far-off land or nearby, travel changes us. Each time we leave home, we learn something new. Travel helps us to understand and accept the differences we have. There are many things that can go wrong when we are away and embracing the joys and difficulties creates resilience. Expand your mind and horizons by taking a trip and challenging your boundaries of comfort.

———

July 18

DREAMS ARE TELLING and can reveal what we wish for. The ability to visualize and see things that have yet to be created is an act of inspiration. When we pay attention to our dreams, there are messages within our subconscious mind. However, staying in our dreams can keep us from reality. Finding balance between what we wish for and what is takes awareness and flexibility. The life we have deserves as much attention as our dreams.

July 19

DURING THE SUMMER, it can feel like everything is bright and sunny. And yet sometimes life can feel like the dead of winter, with nothing happening nor any hope to be found. During these times, it's important to remember that the timing of your life is accurate. Growth and healing don't occur on a linear scale. It's okay if something feels like it's taking longer than expected. Be patient with yourself. The light will return in time.

July 20

THERE IS AWE TO BEHOLD in the simplest pleasures. In the middle of an open field, the sun sets below the endless horizon. The flat expanse makes the sky appear bigger. An endless view of the sunset's changing color plays like an art-filled movie screen. Sky blue merges with gold and rose and eventually fades into deep midnight blue. Gradually the entire sky illuminates with the stars and galaxies and what was once just an open field transforms into a planetarium.

July 21

YOUR FRIENDSHIP IS AN OFFERING of yourself to another. It's a sacred gift to be given and received. Friendship is a magical connection that makes life richer and more enjoyable. Give this gift with openness, grace, and love. There are many people we can be kind to and few we can truly open up to. Treasure the friendships that have enriched your life. Friendship makes life more meaningful and bearable.

———

July 22

A PRIDE IS RULED by a long-maned lion. He is strong, regal, and exudes confidence. He does nothing to gain attention, yet his presence is hard to ignore. Our fellow Leos exude magnetism that draws people in. Their zest for life is expressed in the work they do, the clothes they wear, and their deep love for their family. When we are in the presence of a Leo, we can feel their authentic charm. Offer appreciation to the authentic and confident Leo in your life.

July 23

COURAGE COMES FROM DOING what scares us, despite what others may think. It can mean taking a risk or saying no to what no longer serves us. Courage can look like doing and also being still. Our intuition is our navigator and when we live from our hearts, we have the ability to decide what aligns with our values. Courage is core values in action; it's the generosity to be true to yourself and show up authentically. Knowing yourself well encourages true acts of bravery.

July 24

HEARING THAT EVERYTHING HAPPENS for a reason can feel trite and dismissive. When you look back on your life, notice where trials led to beautiful places that may have been unimaginable. Recognize the detours and where they led. Sometimes our plans are not what they seem. All journeys have a destination and many times getting lost is part of learning more about yourself. Even if it feels like nothing is going well, know that whatever is happening is not forever.

July 25

UNCERTAINTY IS DIFFICULT to embrace. It's natural to want to know how things will turn out. We can feel unmoored by what-ifs and unanswered questions. Having a plan gives us a sense of certainty and control. But this is just a false sense of security. No matter how well we plan, anything can happen and plans can change. Being flexible and open to change helps quell the disappointment of unmet expectations. When you feel the need to know, let go and breathe.

July 26

A VOLCANO ERUPTS WHEN PRESSURE RISES from deep within. As the earth moves, it creates the perfect environment for hot magma to burst through a crack. When we are triggered by something, it can hit a nerve that lies deep within. Sometimes this pressure comes from an unconscious hurt creating a reaction. When you notice a hurt boiling up, pay attention to the pain. Acknowledging the presence of pain reveals the crack where healing can occur.

July 27

OUR STORIES ARE PORTALS into our souls. Sharing
them can help us heal and bring others closer to us. When
we tell our stories, we release the tension that holds the
shame, guilt, grief, and fear within us. When others share
their stories with us, we provide the gift of listening and
acceptance. The telling and listening of stories are offerings
to and from our souls. Trust and connection are nurtured
when we hold space and have space held for us.

July 28

THERE IS A SACRED EMPTINESS that loss creates. The
space where something beautiful once thrived left barren by
departure feels immense. This emptiness is a fertile place
for love to take root if tended with care and the openness to
grieve the loss. Sorrow invites the sacred power of stillness.
Letting go of what once was takes time. Be gentle with
your heart as you heal. Eventually the space will be filled.
Your resilience is a sacred power.

July 29

MOVE YOUR BODY, especially when you feel down. Movement shifts the energy that lies stagnant within our bodies, minds, and souls. Think about a time when you went on a walk. How did you feel after? If you find yourself near the ocean, breathe in the cleansing salt air and feel the power of the waves at your feet. Step outside and feel your feet firmly planted on the ground. Allow nature's energy to help you calm and reset.

———

July 30

RESISTANCE CAUSES PAIN and suffering. When you find yourself at the precipice of growth, it can feel difficult to move through the stages. Growing pains feel like resistance in our body when muscles and bones stretch to their new heights. Eventually things relax as everything adjusts to the change. If you're in the middle of growth and it feels easier to stop, press on. This temporary discomfort is making room for a new level of comfort. You are leveling up.

July 31

SUNFLOWERS TURN THEIR BRIGHT-YELLOW HEADS toward the sun from sunrise to sunset. Each day they soak up every possible sun ray as they grow and mature. Never stooping forward, their strong stalks hold up their flowers and heavy seed discs. These summer blooms are a lovely reminder to look up often and revel in the beauty of the sunshine. Turn your head toward things that are bright and encouraging, especially when things feel gloomy.

August 1

AS YOU ENTER THIS NEW MONTH, repeat these affirmations to yourself: *I am grateful for the warmth of August and the energy that it brings. My appreciation for the summer rises as I begin to notice the slight changes in the trees. I look forward to new memories and good conversations. I am grateful for the joy of connection and friendship. I will bask in the glory of the sun's light and warmth as the days begin to shorten. May this month bring joy and closeness to friendships.*

August 2

GETTING TO KNOW SOMEONE takes time and effort. Small talk can be a good way to break the ice, but relationships grow underneath the surface. Imagine a plant without roots; it would shrivel and dry. Roots allow it to absorb nutrients and water, keeping it healthy and grounded. Our relationships deserve to be tended to by asking deeper questions and getting to know the souls of each other. When relationships are rooted in trust, communication, and deeper understanding, they thrive.

August 3

CHECK IN ON YOUR LOVED ONES, especially the ones who are always doing the checking in. It's easy to take advantage of our loved ones, assuming they will always be there for us. In our world of constant contact and connectivity, we can often dismiss the power of a call or letter. However, these forms of communication are still appreciated and, most times, mean more than a quick text or like on a post. A small gesture of reaching out can strengthen connection and appreciation.

August 4

WHAT IF THE THING THAT YOU THINK IS MOST NEEDED is something you created? Imagine yourself harnessing your bravery to create something from nothing. See what's possible in this vast space of potential. Allow yourself to dream big and notice how it feels to see this need being met by something you created. Then choose to begin. Take one step toward this creation. Take action when the moment strikes. Sometimes our muse comes to visit for only a short while.

August 5

OUR STORIES HOLD POWER. If we share them, we can help others know that they aren't alone, and we can build connections. When we keep the hard ones hidden, they often become a burden filled with shame, guilt, and regret. Even if you're not ready to share, writing down your stories can help you process and heal. Humans have been telling stories for ages. Stories have been the groundwork of connection, community, and the history that we learn from.

August 6

APOLOGIES AND EXPRESSIONS OF LOVE are powerful when genuinely given. Communication can destroy or repair. When a wrong has occurred, ignoring the problem and the other person involved breaks down trust. Speak honestly and compassionately. Being able to admit to wrongdoing is mature and validating to the person who's been wronged. Taking responsibility for your actions isn't always easy, but it opens the door to honesty. Keep the lines of communication open to build up, grow, and repair in love.

August 7

LOOK FOR THE GOOD IN SITUATIONS while also acknowledging the full spectrum of what's occurring. Negative events are stickier in our minds. It takes ten positive events to outweigh one negative event. Gratitude helps us anchor in the good while dealing with the bad. It's a delicate balance of holding two opposing thoughts. Gratitude is saying, "This is happening and also this is true." It's in the "and also" that we can find hope when things feel bleak.

August 8

THERE IS NO NEED TO RUSH the healing of your heart. A heart breaks where love was once the glue. Losing love feels like a death. It's a tender hurt that needs nurturing and time to heal. Give your heart time to process the emotions as they arise. There may be a range of feelings and that's okay. Be kind to yourself as your heart mends. Ask for what you need during this time. Eventually you will love again.

August 9

A LAKE REFLECTS THE SKY. Its waters are nature's mirror. At sunset the lake mirrors the changing colors of the sky as the sun effortlessly dips. As dusk falls the lake remains calm. Eventually the sun will cycle its way back above the lake shining in its reflection. During the cycles of life, it's important to find someone to mirror back our light, especially when times are dark. Think of someone who is steady, like a lake, and who can remind you of your shine.

August 10

FIRE'S ENERGY IS DESTRUCTIVE and purifying. There is a productive side of fire, like warmth and clearing. There is also a destructive side, tearing through towns and forests. Growth can occur after a fire, but if the flames burn unexpectedly, the time to grow back can cause heartache. Often there are two sides to each argument and, like fire, they can clear something up or tear someone down. When fires are stoked in a relationship, be mindful of its course and the time it takes to recover.

August 11

LIFE CAN FEEL LIKE A NEVER-ENDING TRIAL, especially when we feel alone. We can feel stressed by the chaos that occurs. When it feels like there is no more to give, ask for help. We are not meant to do life alone. Connection is an essential human need. It's what gives us meaning, purpose, and joy. Surround yourself with people you trust and love. They will encourage you during hard times and celebrate with you during the good times. Life is meant to be shared.

August 12

LIKE AN EAGLET LEARNING TO FLY, there are many stages to go through before our ideas take flight. At first we go inward and nest, awakening to a new idea. Then we dream and incubate the idea. Taking time to learn more about the topic or path helps us trust the process. Eventually we explore by taking steps toward this change. After stumbling and getting back up like an eaglet, eventually we take the leap that all our stages led us toward. In time the right ideas soar.

August 13

IT'S HARD TO SEE SOMEONE HAVE what you yearn for. Even after acceptance has found its way into your heart, grief slips through the cracks, allowing that yearning to squeeze the heart as a reminder. These heart pangs are for the loss of what could have been as it felt so beautiful and real. In time the waves of yearning will pass. Welcome the feelings and let them flow through you. Eventually your heart will feel stronger.

August 14

TWILIGHT OCCURS IN STAGES. When the sun sets, the sky progressively darkens. First rose and sepia hues wash across the sky. Then lavender and navy begin to set in, and the first visible stars appear. Finally darkness deepens, and night begins to fall. Constellations and galaxies materialize the darker the sky becomes. When we become aware, the changing colors can enchant. Being mindful helps us to notice the subtle and fascinating changes in nature.

August 15

WHEN WE CALIBRATE OUR HEARTS toward love, we begin to see the good in others. Everyone has good and bad things about themselves. No one is perfect. Love is a kind and nurturing presence that welcomes acceptance. We feel safer in the company of love. Love helps us open up more and share our stories more easily. Love allows us to show up for others and show others our vulnerabilities. Value the relationships in your life and choose to love often.

August 16

WHEN YOUR SOUL YEARNS for meaning, listen for the answers that are found within. Often the discomfort of not knowing leads us toward distraction. We quiet the inner yearning because it's uncomfortable to feel. Discomfort can lead us to reach for our favorite ways to distract ourselves when what our soul really needs is quiet. Take some time to search for answers and let your intuition speak. Then when big questions arise, your intuition will feel like a trusted and dear friend.

August 17

THE OCEAN MOVES sending ripples and waves along the shore. Our efforts can create great movements in our lives. Sometimes intentions don't always go as planned. We can put in great effort, and yet, things still don't work out. There is a reason for the failure, even if it's not immediately apparent. In time what is meant to occur will begin to arise, like the swells of a wave washing debris from the shoreline.

August 18

THINK ABOUT THE VASTNESS OF THE OCEAN. Imagine you are standing on the shore looking out into the horizon. What seems like the end of the world is just the beginning of the sea. On the other side of this great expanse may be another person looking out at the expanse from their direction. What feels like the end is only a continuation of the connectedness of the planet. We are all connected.

August 19

OUR BODIES HOLD THE POWER to give us clues to what it needs. However, many of us are so deep in our heads that we forget to check in with our physical needs. Staying trapped in our thoughts neglects our body's clues. Spending time to tap into listening to our bodies can help hone our attention to our physical intuition. In time we will feel things that need attention. This may be uncomfortable at first, and yet, the discomfort is an invitation to heal.

———

August 20

TAKE A MOMENT FOR MINDFULNESS. As you allow yourself to settle into stillness, notice what you see. Take in the colors and shapes with your eyes. Then notice what you can hear nearby and far away. Remembering to breathe, notice what you can smell. Then focus on what you can feel—the texture of what you're sitting on, your clothes, and the air around you. Finally notice what you can taste. As you slowly focus on your senses, you have allowed yourself a moment of mindfulness.

August 21

ROAMING CAN LEAD US NOWHERE, and sometimes that's the point. Always knowing which direction to take and following a map can rob us from serendipity and trusting our instincts. Sometimes wandering leads us to beautiful vistas, waterfalls, and even community. When you're feeling restless or aimless, take a walk. Roam through your neighborhood or hike a new trail. Allow movement to shift your energy. Be open to the journey, even if it leads you back home.

———

August 22

UNCERTAINTY FUELS THE ANXIOUS FIRES within. Like a moth to a flame, fear hovers where anxiety looms. Gratitude can quell the desire to stoke the flames of worry. When we are focusing on scarcity and uncertainty, we allow our minds to worry about things we don't have any control over. Gratitude shifts our focus from what's wrong to what's going well. When we stop and recognize the good and what we do have, our mindset shifts and our energy changes.

August 23

A JOB WELL DONE, or a garden well-tended, Virgos work
so hard to create order and beauty. They are reliable and
see things that many pass over. Natural detectives, their
attention to detail is exacting. They discern well, while
many may go back and forth on decisions. They can read a
room and notice needs before many realize they have them.
Their devotion to beauty and order makes our lives run
more smoothly. Appreciate the devoted and caring Virgo in
your life.

———

August 24

YOUR ABILITY TO REFINE and perfect brings order to
the outer world. You are devoted to the causes and people
who found a place in your heart. You work hard to make
the world a better place. And yet, your greatest work is the
releasing of control and allowing things to fall into place.
Let go of the urge to fix. Embrace surrender. There is
nothing that you need to do to be deserving. You are worthy
of just being.

August 25

FINDING FLOW COMES WHEN WE ARE CONSUMED
with something and time passes without notice. Entering
the flow state is where creation thrives. Ideas take shape
when our mind is focused without distraction. Our minds
are capable of amazing feats. Whether it's writing, painting,
cooking, building, or knitting, flow brings us into a state of
timelessness. Consider a time when the minutes passed
without notice and you felt alive. Make space for these
activities to welcome flow into your days.

———

August 26

IN THE HILLS ABOVE THE SAN FRANCISCO BAY the scent
of eucalyptus drifts through the air. It's an unmistakable
scent that is green, herbaceous, and calming, and not far from
the hustle of the cities below. Walking through the trees with
the breeze flowing is an adventure for the senses. Different
scents are helpful to help soothe and calm our nervous
system and even invoke good memories. Spend a moment to
recall a scented memory, feeling a calm rise in your heart.

August 27

WHEN DISCONTENT FLOODS IN, identify what you need and ask for it. Find someone trustworthy and share your needs with them. Knowing what you want can help quell the overwhelm of discontent. Sometimes unhappiness is a sign to pause and discover what's lacking. It can also be an invitation to notice and remember the goodness in your life. Whether you need something or to be reminded of life's goodness, take time to uncover the message your soul is sending.

———

August 28

THERE IS A VAST AMOUNT TO LEARN. Living with a growth mindset will help to overcome hardships, seize opportunities, and make deeper connections. Learning promotes change, which leads to growth. The ability and willingness to change opens one up to wisdom. Notice when you feel resistant to learning something new or different. Resistance shows up when comfort is threatened. However, on the other side of resistance and comfort is acceptance and growth. Insights await you.

August 29

THE LIGHT AT THE END OF THE DAY softens as the sun sets. It's a lovely reminder to notice where softening can be welcomed in our lives. It's easy to harden when fights and frustrations occur. We can see something in the news that creates doubt in the belief of the good in humanity. These worries harden our hearts. And yet, nature reminds us to soften and allow opening to occur. Let go of the stories and frustrations and welcome ease each evening.

———

August 30

SPEAK TO YOURSELF as you would your dearest friend or a sweet child. Offer yourself the nurturing you so desperately long for. Spending our days waiting for another to fill the gap in our hearts will leave us frustrated and disillusioned. Turning inward and offering the care and love that's most needed is like water to parched soil. Soon the seeds of comfort, thriving, and compassion will bloom. Keep watering your soul's garden. Your blooms are as important as any others.

August 31

EVERYTHING THRIVES UNDER THE SUN as it rises and sets each day. As the earth rotates around the sun, it experiences seasons, changes in temperature, and cycles of maturation. It's amazing that a giant star influences so many vital parts of our lives. Every day, we have an opportunity to welcome growth and joy. Take a moment to pause and thank the sun. Spend some time basking underneath its magnificent light.

September 1

END YOUR BUSY DAY BY REPEATING these affirmations to yourself: *I am grateful for the unknown because it provides a sense of wonder. I open my mind to discovering new things and finding new people to connect with. Looking back, I see that the answers I was seeking appeared exactly when I needed them. I'm grateful for the patience I've gained through embracing the unknown. I release my grasp from needing to know and am reminded of the depth of gratitude that accompanies a long-awaited answer.*

September 2

GIVE YOUR BODY COMPASSION when your mind points out perceived flaws. Recognize the distances your feet have walked and the miles your legs have moved you. Praise each wrinkle for its evidence of a life lived. Inhale deeply into your belly and marvel at its capacity to expand with breath. Look at your hands and think about each embrace and all the work they've done. Offer thanks for your body as you appreciate everything it's done for you.

September 3

BEGIN, EVEN IF YOU DON'T FEEL READY. The beauty of beginnings is the potential that lies ahead. Fear keeps us from moving forward toward the things that are important to us. It's very possible that we will fail at the beginning, and that is scary. Failure doesn't feel good, and yet, it's inevitable when starting something new. Having a beginner's mind allows us to show up and absorb new information. You are resilient and you are able to get back up and try again.

September 4

BE GENTLE WITH YOURSELF when sadness visits. Don't push the feeling away for it will eventually return. Feel what needs to be felt. Even though it would be amazing to feel great all the time, life throws us curveballs that cause emotions to rise. Pay attention to what your body is saying. Be still and tend to your emotional needs. This storm will pass and when the clouds break, the sun will rise and set once more.

———

September 5

ANSWERS REVEAL THEMSELVES when the time is right. Our urge to have them revealed whenever we want invites worry. Waiting calls us to be still. Give time to silence and stillness in order to hear the answers that you seek. Eventually you will be able to press forward with clarity and confidence knowing that answers arrive when the timing is right. In this pause, breathe a little deeper. Welcome calm while you wait to take action. Soon enough you'll be on your way.

September 6

TRYING HARD FOR SOMETHING TO WORK TAKES RESOLVE. Sometimes the things we work so hard for never take place. The thing we want most can at times be an elusive hope when it never occurs, such as a woman's desire to become pregnant. She can take every measure possible and yet never conceive. As heartbreak sets in, acceptance feels far from reach. Love and support will see you through the dark stages of grief. Releasing a dream takes time. Wanting something that was an idea rooted in the heart is evidence of love.

———

September 7

DEEP INSIDE A CAVE pitch black envelops and can almost be felt. Rock walls seem to close in and the dark feels heavy. It's a claustrophobic sensation that only light and air can relieve. Sometimes the trials in life can feel like a dark cave. Relief feels unattainable when difficulties surround us. A desire for a breather is predominant. When the feelings of being suffocated by troubles arise, remember to breathe. Breath relieves and calms the nervous system, eventually welcoming ease.

September 8

GO OUTSIDE AND EXPLORE the natural world. It's easy to get caught up in the many distractions available to us. We live in a world filled with screens and artificial lights. And yet, the sun puts on a show every day as it rises and sets. Trees that have been standing longer than we've been alive offer shade and grounding energy. Oceans lap toward the shore delivering gifts of shells and cleaning the sand. There is beauty to behold every day.

September 9

MOMENTS OF PEACE ARE HEALING and insightful because the answers you seek are within you. But sometimes it's really hard to find them because our minds go all over the place and allow fear to be the dominant voice. When we stop letting fear direct our lives, it's amazing what can transpire. Uncovering the blocks that keep us frozen in place takes time. We can then take the steps to move forward. Stillness is the fertile ground where answers appear.

September 10

TAKING A RISK REQUIRES BRAVERY. There are no guarantees to the chances we take but there are lessons to be learned. When an opportunity arises, it's important to weigh the possible outcomes. Part of harnessing your bravery is checking in with your gut and asking whether it's fear or excitement, as they can feel the same. Fear is a gift that wants to keep us safe but can often override potential joy. Courage lives in the possibilities.

September 11

WHEN GRIEF APPEARS, it stays with us, coming and going when least expected. Learning to live with sorrow requires honoring its presence in your life. We are able to access more compassion, empathy, and love after grief occurs. Grief can help us open our hearts because it's a testament to our capacity to love. It's also true that we grow around our grief. When grief appears, welcome it in, feel what it has to show you about yourself and thank it for the deeper access to your heart.

September 12

TIDES CONTINUALLY RISE AND FALL. At low tide, what was once underwater reveals a stretch of beach and rocks where seaweed, crabs, and sand dollars can be found. As the tide rises, the beach disappears and the rocks and sand become submerged. Creatures living in the tidal zone are adaptable to the rise and fall of the tides. Like tides, life offers constant change with highs and lows. There is strength and resilience available in learning to adapt.

September 13

FEELING OVERWORKED CAN CREATE RESENTMENT. When we don't take breaks, our nervous system can feel overwhelmed. Although deadlines are important, it's just as important to take care of ourselves. The days of hustle and burnout are ending. The more science studies the nervous system and mindfulness, the more we understand the detrimental effects of stress. If you're feeling overwhelmed and overworked, try to invite pockets of peace into your day. Take breaks and honor your nervous system through breath and meditation.

September 14

CONTROL KEEPS US FROM RECEIVING the goodness that is on its way. When we are in our heads trying to make sure everything is falling into place, we can miss wonderful things that are right in front of us. The need to control is like a horse with blinders and a bit, unable to see all around and potentially go off course. Flow is able to enter our lives when we release the intoxicating pull of a sense of false control.

September 15

PAUSE AND NOTICE how the clouds slowly move and dissipate. As they float through the sky, their shapes continually transform. At sunset they glow with the final rays of the day's sunlight, offering depth to the sky's expanse. Watching clouds brings a moment of mindfulness into the day and also reminds us that nothing is permanent. Allow your thoughts to flow like the clouds in the sky. Let them change shape as you figure things out.

September 16

WITHIN EACH OF US IS A GALAXY of wisdom waiting to be explored. As we go through life, we collect stars of knowledge that accumulate into our inner galaxy. Take a moment to think about your life's path. Notice the pitfalls and joys that you've encountered. Try to see how each event offered you a glimpse of wisdom through the lessons learned. Then close your eyes and imagine all these stars colliding creating a beautiful galaxy within you.

September 17

YOU ARE WORTHY. Don't run away from the goodness that's trying to enter your life. When we feel unworthy, it can be difficult to open up to abundance and joy. Deflecting goodness is a message from your soul, an invitation to address this insecurity that is rooted deep within. There are messages all over telling us that we need to earn love and goodness. Let go of the urge to prove yourself and open your hands to receive what's on its way to you.

September 18

THE OCEAN HOLDS GREAT POWER and stirs awe in those who are near it. Massive waves occur in the middle of the ocean where only a few may witness. The ocean doesn't need a large audience to express its might and magnificence. It constantly rises and falls as if taking a bow for her amazing feats. We need the ocean for the health of our planet. When you are in its presence, treat it with respect and honor its role in the balance it creates.

September 19

THE SUNSET IS A SYMBOL of completion, a turning of a page. The day's end is a time for reflection, a closing of a chapter in your life. Each day is only one part of the whole story of your life. You are on your hero's journey and there will be initiations, adventures, and eventually a return to yourself. Each day holds lessons, joys, and surprises. Let today be whatever it was meant to be. Your next chapter begins in the morning.

September 20

YOU DON'T HAVE TO DO EVERYTHING on your own. Let others help you. It can be hard to accept help, especially when you're so capable, but you're not here to do life alone. Let others in. Show your tender spots to those you trust. Allow them to step in and be a part of your life. Accept help when it's offered, especially if you are often the one who helps. We are born to connect with others.

———

September 21

AT THE END OF EACH SEASON, we have the opportunity to look back with gratitude. When the new season begins, we can look forward to new plans and dreams. Our intentions set the tone for how we move through life. Taking time to reflect and plan ahead is an intentional act of mindful living. Perhaps all the goals won't come to fruition, but the intention will help move us forward and see lessons in letting go of what wasn't meant to be.

September 22

THE WORLD IS MORE PEACEFUL when things are fair and diplomatic. Our fellow Libras are peace loving and know how to connect. They will weigh all the options to make sure everyone involved is enjoying themselves and feels seen. Their love flows freely to those fortunate enough to be their friends and family. They see you and find beauty and goodness in each person. Being in their presence feels like a warm hug. Appreciate the peace-loving and thoughtful Libras in your life.

September 23

AS YOU STRIVE TO SEEK BALANCE, be sure to be kind to yourself. Things won't always be fair and your peace may be disrupted from time to time. You don't need to make things better; you can let them be. Remember that life is cyclical and that sometimes things will feel unpredictable. Things fall into place in their own time. If mistakes occur, offer your heart compassion and move on. There is always another chance to try again.

September 24

A MARINE LAYER HUGS THE AREAS NEAR THE SEA early in the morning. This eerie pocket of clouds hovers over the land and sea until late morning or early afternoon. Depending on perception, it can be a welcome reprieve from the sun or a gloomy start to a day. Each day invites us to choose to see things in a positive or negative light. How we choose to interpret things will set the tone for our days.

September 25

WANTING THINGS TO HAPPEN a certain way can keep us from experiencing the flow of life. Like a beaver building a dam on a river, we block what's meant to occur. In time a river finds its way regardless of what blocks it. Invite ease into your life by releasing your grip. Gently remind yourself to accept not knowing what will happen. Open to the unexpected. There is magic in the hidden surprises life has to offer.

September 26

THE INNER CRITIC KEEPS US FROM ENJOYING LIFE.
It hides the incredible things that are happening by criticizing
and judging ourselves and others. When we listen to this
voice, we start to believe the negativity it provides. Paying
attention to it feeds it. But if we notice the inner critic, we
can choose to redirect it to something more positive.
With practice, criticisms and judgments will lose the
power they once had and our minds will be honed for
seeking what's good.

———

September 27

GRATITUDE UNVEILS DEEPER JOY. There are many small
things that go unnoticed—the small rocks of different colors
in a riverbed, a bee landing on a colorful flower, a bird in a
tree building a nest are all small things that don't beg for
attention. When we practice gratitude, we are more likely to
notice these small joys. As we begin to notice the delights
in our every day, gratitude wells up within. The smallest
appreciation feeds the heart's capacity for joy.

September 28

IT'S OKAY TO TAKE SOME TIME TO HEAL. Your timeline won't match the expectations of others. Sink into the stillness of healing and pay attention to your needs. Be gentle with yourself as you mend. You'll find your way once again, but for now, just be where you need to be. Endings are a call for healing and renewal. Morning comes after a long night. But in this moment of sunset on whatever may be ending, let yourself feel all that needs feeling.

———

September 29

WHEN THE SUN SETS during a storm, the sky quickly goes dark. The radiant colors that usually accompany a sunset fail to appear as the clouds and rain immerse the sky. Even though it feels as though the sun's warmth is weaker during a storm, it's still powerfully holding center, creating gravity for life to thrive. During life's storms, our intuition is our center point, like the sun, navigating us toward thriving. Be still to hear what you need during these times.

September 30

IT'S COMMON TO WANT TO KNOW the answers and how things will work out. Finding answers would be easier if we had a treasure map where X marks the spot. If we could see where the path led, perhaps the unknown wouldn't feel so daunting. And yet, this time of discovery is a treasure hunt toward deeper knowing and understanding. Once you begin the trek, you will never be the same. Notice the treasure hidden in this unfamiliar territory. You will emerge changed.

October 1

OFFER YOURSELF SOME KINDNESS by repeating these affirmations to yourself: *I am grateful for endings and the promise of new beginnings. As my heart releases one thing, it creates room for something new. I honor the emotions that come up as I let go and wait patiently for healing to occur. Although the process may take some time, I offer myself love and compassion. As I notice hope sprouting once again in my heart, I recognize the growth that is taking place in what was once an empty space with deep gratitude.*

October 2

EVERYTHING EVENTUALLY CHANGES. Babies grow up to be adults, seasons change, and saplings grow to giant trees. Life is full of beginnings and endings. Transformations are often hard to embrace, especially when we've become comfortable with the way things are. It can feel disorienting to undergo transitions. But during these times we are learning new things and gaining wisdom. As we grow in wisdom, we are better equipped to offer empathy and understanding. Stay open and embrace the beauty of perspective.

October 3

A HIKER CAN FEEL A SENSE of exhilaration when she sees what seems to be the end of the trail ahead. As she approaches, she notices that it is only a turn, a false summit. This can cause frustration and even despair. False summits feel difficult as the relief of completion is anticipated. Life can feel like a continuous climb, and yet, at each turn, we can stop and appreciate the progress that has been made. Each step is a destination.

October 4

ALLOWING YOURSELF TO FALL IN LOVE again after heartbreak is an act of courage. When you decide to let someone in, you open up the most vulnerable places within yourself to them. It's inviting intimacy where self-protection once thrived. Even though you may be hurt again, you can always come back to your heart. Your heart is the root of your courage. Each relationship brings lessons and invites us to grow together. In this space, we can recognize the strength and courage of our spirit.

October 5

A GROUP OF PEOPLE stand on the shore, watching the setting sun dip into the ocean. They wait with hopeful eyes to see if the sun will disappear with a green flash. The sun looks like it's flattening as it gets closer to the horizon. The atmosphere is clear, creating the perfect conditions for the illusion of a flash. At the final moment of sunset, the sun disappears with a final spark of green. Nature is full of stunning surprises for those who look for them.

———

October 6

HAVING TO MAKE DECISIONS can leave us frozen in our tracks. Wanting to make the right choice can keep us stuck in analysis. Reviewing choices over and over causes stress, making the decision even more difficult. Life is full of forks in the road where we are faced with decisions. Trust your instinct and seek wise counsel if needed. The beauty of choice is that we can begin again and get back up if we fail. Nothing is permanent.

October 7

CHOOSING LOVE WHEN FACED WITH OPPOSITION is hard to do. It's natural to react and defend, especially when feeling threatened. Reactions based in fear only perpetuate the problem. Fear will keep us ready to fight, while love will soften our hearts and open our minds. Try responding with love and stay calm. Take deep breaths to soothe your nerves when fear takes over. Choose to soften when situations invite hardening. See how love opens the door to understanding and resolution.

October 8

JOY IS AVAILABLE EVEN WHEN life feels like a storm. It's easy to find the good when things are positive, and it feels like everything's falling into place. It's during hard times that we need to utilize our spiritual tool kits. Each day offers small moments of joy and gratitude. They can be as simple as a piece of delicious fruit or seeing a bird fly by. This doesn't take away from the gravity of life's hardships but helps us weather inevitable storms that occur.

October 9

AS TREES AND FRUIT MATURE, they reveal their true colors. Maples turn from vibrant greens to fiery reds. Grapes become more full and deeper in color as they ripen on the vine. The riper the fruit, the more complex the flavor. Maturity offers the depth of knowledge and strength of survival. As we age, our true colors begin to show up. Our resilience breeds wisdom and strength of spirit. Embrace each age and the complexity it provides. Maturation is fascinating.

October 10

WIND HAS THE POWER to move sand across the desert and water into a towering wave. It spreads pollen and seeds helping them find new places to land. It's welcomed on a hot day and whistles through the icy trees of winter. The wind plays gently across our skin and in our hair, reminding us how everything is impermanent and to let go. Holding on only creates tension. Be like the wind and let things fall where they may.

October 11

TIME DOESN'T HEAL ALL WOUNDS, but it provides space for integration and perspective. When pain is acute, it feels like there's no end to grief. Our minds obsess about what happened and we can't imagine how to move forward. Eventually there is a fading to the sensitivity around the wound and scar tissue forms. A reminder of the hurt is evident but fades over time. If you're in the beginning phase of hurt, give yourself time to process. Soon enough your strength will return.

October 12

A TINY ACORN holds a wealth of knowledge. Within these fruits is the wisdom to become mighty oaks. Something so small is quite important to the life of a forest. When you feel like you don't have anything of value to contribute, consider how you hold a wealth of knowledge. Deep inside are roots of wisdom from your experiences, learnings, and intuition. Sometimes it only takes one word or thought to change the course of a meeting or connection.

October 13

HIGH ROCK WALLS CREATE a canyon where a river flows through. For centuries, the same river carved through the canyon revealing layers of rock. A hiker walks through looking up at the sheer magnificence of the water's power. An echo reverberates through the canyon reflecting their words back to them. They are filled with awe and wonder at nature's grandeur. Think of something that fills you with a sense of wonder. Close your eyes, breathe deep, and offer gratitude for the experience.

October 14

TRAVELING WHEN YOU'RE YOUNG helps you see the world with fresh eyes. Experience from a place of newness with an open mind, climb mountains, sleep on the ground, meet new friends, and try new foods. Explore and feel your mind expand. Traveling when you're older helps you view the world with a deeper understanding. You can then feel the essence of the place, connect deeper, and return to places that once grabbed your heart. No matter your age, allow travel to move your soul.

October 15

THE PAST IS A TEACHER and the future is a dream. The ability to be right here, right now, is a practice. When lessons or dreams seek attention in the present moment, acknowledge their presence. Let the worries flow away. Release attachment to outcomes of the past and potential future and breathe into this moment. Notice something lovely in your surroundings. Pay attention to your breath. Be grateful for the quiet moment you have created for yourself.

October 16

OFFER LOVE TO THE PEOPLE IN YOUR LIFE. It takes time and effort to build trust. When we trust someone, we can communicate needs and how we prefer to be loved. Love is a flower for us to bloom and grow. If properly tended, it can mature into something quite beautiful. Think about the people in your life. Who do you trust and love? Offer them love in the ways they want to receive love. Show them you care and pay attention. Love generates love.

October 17

SURROUND YOURSELF WITH PEOPLE you can be yourself around. Trust the ones who show up for the big and small parts of life. Love the ones who share their hearts and stay open, even when life is hard. Appreciate the ones who have something to teach you. Forgive the ones who are truly sorry. Offer grace to the ones who are in a painful season and need extra time and space. Find the ones who help you grow into who you're meant to be.

———

October 18

GET CURIOUS ABOUT LIFE, especially when it feels like nothing is working out. In times of dead ends and missed turns, we can find new vistas and even realize the detour was meant to be. It's easy to get so caught up in our plans and goals that we can miss possible redirection. When things don't work out, it can be a way to redirect focus toward what is supposed to happen. Sometimes what feels like a wrong turn brings the greatest surprises.

October 19

IMAGINE SITTING BY A MOUNTAIN STREAM. The sound of water gurgling past the rocks soothes you. The constant lapping of water from the bank that's never dry harmonizes with the bird songs above. The breeze lightly grazes your skin; the air is cool, and the sun is warm. For a moment, nature's symphony can have us forget all of life's struggles. Where can you remember feeling a deep sense of peace? You can return to this memory often, especially when you're in need of soothing.

October 20

SENSITIVE HEARTS ARE OPEN to feeling the entire range of emotions. Their joy feels like climbing to a mountaintop and their sorrows are as deep as the sea. The capacity to really tap into feelings is a gift. Nurture your sensitive heart with compassion and grace. Take the time needed to repair and restore for energy seeps in easier through your softness. It's a beautiful thing to stay open in a world where it's easier to shut down.

October 21

AMBIGUOUS LOSS LEAVES MANY QUESTIONS unanswered and can make grieving unbearable. Living in the questions leaves little room for comfort. The questions are part of the process and even if the answers never appear, allowing space to grieve what could have been is healing. Hope returns unexpectedly over time. Eventually the sun's warmth is welcomed, as is the hug of a friend. Tears are the physical manifestation of grieving and loving what could have been. Be gentle with yourself as you heal.

October 22

LIFE EXPANDS AND CONTRACTS, offering us the chance to shine and retreat. When life is expansive and amazing things are happening, offer gratitude for the opportunities. When life is hard and you feel like contracting and hiding away, offer gratitude for a home to retreat to. No matter whether life feels expansive or restricted, your light continues to glow from within. If we were always shining, we would eventually burn out. Embrace the times of shine and of dimming.

October 23

CRAWLING ACROSS THE ARID EXPANSE of a desert, a scorpion persists, carrying her young on her back. She's strategic as she finds her way, calling upon her inner power to make it to her destination. Loyal to those she loves, she will do anything to protect them. Our fellow Scorpios are fighters as well, standing up for the people they love and the causes they care for. They are quiet but dynamic in their power. Appreciate the strategic and loyal Scorpio in your life.

October 24

TRUE INTIMACY REQUIRES BEING OPEN enough to dive into the depths with another. Deep relationships thrive with intimacy. When we decide to truly know another person well, we see both good and bad. It's a powerful skill to be able to see a whole person and offer them love, forgiveness, trust, and a piece of your heart. Choose who you share your life with wisely. The right partner will help you grow and love you for who you are.

October 25

PURSUE THAT WHICH MOVES YOUR SOUL. Explore these things and find ways to incorporate them into your life. When we feed our souls, we become more driven and fulfilled. If there is a cause that stirs your heart, volunteer, give, or learn more about how you can help. Often these are places where our own hearts have been broken. We can make something beautiful out of our sorrows. Our lights shine through where our hearts once cracked.

October 26

DON'T BE HARD ON YOURSELF when mistakes are made. They are stepping stones on life's path. Sometimes mistakes lead to insights that are hidden, begging to be found. Other times mistakes are exactly what need to happen to take us off a path we swore was the right one but actually led to a dead end. Maybe mistakes are just part of being human. Be kind when it feels like something goes wrong. You're doing your best and that's enough.

October 27

SOFTEN INTO THE SOOTHING rhythm of doing nothing. Let your mind rest from all the overthinking. Gently let your body sink into the restorative lull of rest. Let out a full-body exhale. Feel tension melt away as you loosen your grip. There is no need to control or fix. Open your fingers one by one and let it all slip away. Breathe in calm, breathe out everything else. Be soft. It's okay to surrender.

October 28

TO BE THE SHOULDER someone cries on is a great honor. Knowing that there is someone who is trustworthy to share the darkest recesses of our minds with relieves the shadow of isolation that depression casts. When sorrow descends on the soul, it feels too heavy to reach through. Asking for help feels like wading through quicksand. Almost everything feels impossible. Being there for someone is the rope that can rescue the drowning and save a life.

October 29

WHEAT SWAYS GENTLY in the wind. Its yellow stalks look like waves across the open prairie. The wind whispers through the field, rustling the dry leaves ready to be harvested. After a long season of work, the field produces grain and sustenance for the coming months. Hard work pays off, but sometimes it takes time to see the results. Think about harvest season when you're in a period of waiting. Do what you can while you wait. Over time it all comes together.

October 30

WHEN LIFE GETS MESSY, take a deep breath. Things may not fall into place for quite some time. Worrying about things will only augment the issue. Even though the tendency is to clean up messes as soon as possible, allow time to clear things up as needed. Rushing the process will only cause more stress. Remember your breath and release the urge to know the outcome. Embrace not knowing, understanding that the answers are on their way.

October 31

CROWS CALL OUT TO EACH OTHER, cawing from tree to tree. They communicate loudly and often. There is an ancient belief that crows are an indication of passing. These black birds ominously show up to signal that an ending has occurred. Grief feels like a messenger cloaking the griever in darkness delivering a message to process a passing. Allow the tears to fall, call out for support, communicate as loudly as you need to. Grief needs a witness as it honors the ending of something significant.

November 1

AS YOU HONOR WHERE YOU ARE in your journey, repeat these affirmations to yourself: *I am grateful for the natural cycles that life provides. The tides are a reminder of the power of the seas. I bear witness to time passing through the cycles of the moon. Each day the sun reminds me that nothing is permanent as it rises and sets. I will honor where I am right now and recognize that it's only a moment in the cycle of my life. I am grateful for these reminders and witness this moment in time with wonder.*

———

November 2

OUR JOURNEYS CAN INSPIRE others going through similar experiences. When we share from a place of growth and encouragement, we can make a difference. Whether it's one-on-one, online, or in a group, your story holds power. The most important person it helps is you. Finding meaning and perspective are healing balms for the soul. If you're not ready to share your story with others, write it down for your own inspiration. See how far you've come and celebrate your journey.

November 3

ARGUMENTS CAN CREATE SEPARATION and can also open the doors to healing. When a disagreement occurs, it signals that something is off in the relationship. Underneath the stubbornness and need to win is a pain that desires soothing. Sometimes the pain can be healed through having a difficult discussion and opening up to making a change. Wanting to be right and to win can stop the flow of love. Breathe into the tension and look for the opening where healing can begin.

November 4

LOVE LOOKS LIKE sitting next to you when grief takes over. It's the hand that you hold when life feels anxious. Love is calling to check in just to see how you're doing. It shows up and celebrates you when you've accomplished something big or small. Love waits for you to be ready and is kind when you're not. It gives without expecting anything in return or keeping score. Love is the warmth you feel when surrounded by understanding and connection.

November 5

THERE ARE HIDDEN GIFTS that spring forth from the sorrows we have known. Letting go of something that you once loved or deeply wanted is heartbreaking. And yet, room is made for something else to show up. Eventually a spring breaks through a mountain, offering water rich in minerals. The water from the break is often the most desired. Even though we may never forget the things that seemingly break us, our hearts have the capacity to expand where the break occurred.

November 6

IT'S HARD TO FEEL IGNORED. When you have a truth that people deny or refuse to validate, it can create deep resentment and shame. Shame thrives in the dark. Healing comes from having someone shine a light in the deeper recesses of our soul. Finding someone to trust to process things with is like having a lantern held up to guide the way toward healing. We don't need everyone to validate us, just a few we trust to illuminate the way to wholeness.

November 7

IN THE EVENING light hits differently as the sun lowers in the sky. Shadows merge with the horizon and dust motes dance in the light. There is a softness to the evening. The day is coming to an end as work and projects are set aside. Sighs of relief are exhaled. Look at how the light plays in your home throughout the day. Pay attention to how it highlights and contrasts. Take in this simple pleasure of noticing light.

November 8

WHEN IT FEELS LIKE YOU'RE IN A FREE FALL and things don't make sense, find something or someone to help ground you. Grounding energy can be found in stones, trees, or a dear friend. You don't always have to have it together. Sometimes life is hard and it's okay to reach out for support. In the frantic anxiety that comes with the loss of control, hold on to the things that remind you to breathe and that all will be well.

November 9

FIND THE PLACES, people, and things that bring softness out of you. Notice where your soul feels free and floats like a bird on an airstream. Recognize the people who make your heart flutter like a butterfly. Wear the clothes that let you relax and feel comfortable in your skin. Embrace the movement that allows you to express your body in ways that feel nourishing. There is grace and beauty that can only be found when we melt into softness.

———

November 10

THE FIRE WITHIN YOU IS UNIQUE and drives you toward your desires. A fire that is well tended burns long and bright. It radiates heat and provides warmth. Observe how your desires show up. What fuels you to make things happen? What stokes the flames of your dreams? Allow yourself to step toward the things you want. Shine bright like a well-tended flame. Radiate like the heat of the sun. Let yourself become fulfilled and stop hiding from your destiny.

November 11

A TRAGEDY CAN BRING PEOPLE CLOSER together even if there was once a separation. The perspective of hardships can show us what's truly important in life. Communities gather to help each other and give aid where needed. Helping hands and open hearts show the compassionate nature of our souls. Even though terrible things occur, they show us our capacity toward kindness and generosity of spirit. There is healing available to our broken hearts and beauty amid ruin.

November 12

HOPE RETURNS SLOWLY after a period of sadness. Eventually evidence of hope appears. It can be seen in the morning, arising without tears or the desire to be with friends. Hope shows up in connection and the prayers of gratitude. As our hearts thaw from sorrow, we begin to move toward things we once loved. We begin to move our bodies again in ways that feel nourishing. Hope arrives even when we aren't looking. Like magic we feel our hearts warm up to life once more.

November 13

DURING TWILIGHT stars start to appear. It's common to make a wish on the first visible star of the evening. Imagine you are standing underneath the twilight sky and notice the first glimmer of a star. Think of something you'd like to wish for. How does this thing make you feel? Breathe in that feeling and then send your wish out into the universe. Then say thank you for whatever is on its way to you.

———

November 14

THE STORIES WE TELL OURSELVES affect the way we relate to others. Harsh judgments cause separation. Fear creates false narratives. Often these stories aren't true and are perpetuated by believing our perceptions without seeking clarity. If there is a story that keeps repeating in your mind, pause and ask if it's true. If doubts persist, seek the truth by asking questions. Clearing the air can heal a lot of assumptions and create deeper connections.

November 15

A PIONEER TRAVERSES unknown territory to find a place to call home. They deal with various discomforts as they fight their way toward a new way of being and living. When they find their new home, there is a settling in. As we meditate we are like a pioneer traversing the unknown territory of quiet and stillness. At first the journey feels frustrating and awkward. Eventually a new level of comfort is found as we settle down and come home to ourselves.

———

November 16

DURING TIMES OF WAITING, patience may seem elusive. Trying to wait for answers or things to occur causes anticipatory excitement and anxiety. We can feel excited and anxious at the same time, often confusing the two. Patience is a calming salve for these uncertain times. It helps us disregard clocks and calendars. It's the voice of reason when the mind wanders into the chaotic waters of anxiety. It gently whispers: rest here and wait, all will be well in due time.

November 17

VINES CURL AND MAKE THEIR WAY up a wall and through a field. They grow, reaching for the sun with their thin tendrils. No wall is too high or field too long; if allowed to, a vine will go wild. The expansive nature of a vine is a gentle reminder to keep reaching, even though the dream seems far away. The journey may not look like the original dream, but the growth that occurs along the way is invaluable. Keep reaching and let your dreams run wild.

November 18

THINKING ABOUT ALL THE THINGS that could go wrong steals attention from the present moment. There are surprises all around us to be enjoyed, but only if we are open and aware of them. Our minds keep us from this awareness when we are stuck ruminating and regretting. When you find worry creeping in, stop to breathe. Notice something around you. Take in the sights and sounds that surround you. This moment of noticing will redirect your attention from worry to beauty.

November 19

THE UNIVERSE IS VAST and full of ways to support you. The air we breathe is abundant and constantly circulating. Water cycles through clouds and oceans, replenishing supply and offering life to plants and animals. The forests provide oxygen and majesty to behold, to calm our minds and hearts. There are countless ways in which the universe supports you. Open up to see the vast support available to you. Offer gratitude for the ways support flows to you each day.

November 20

TEARS ARE A POWERFUL RELEASE. They can help us alleviate pain held within our minds and bodies. They can help us spiritually release tension from the ambiguity of life. Like rain after atmospheric pressure, tears can soften what has become rigid from holding on. Rain can split open the ground, creating an environment to plant after a period of drought. Before healing and growth can occur, a release is sometimes needed to clear what failed to thrive.

November 21

KNOWING WHEN IT'S TIME to leave can be difficult to face. After putting in a lot of effort, it can be heartbreaking to know something must end. Expiration dates occur over time. Sometimes we ignore the signs to stay within our comfort zone. Leaving can lift your gaze toward possibility where despair loomed. Leaving can reveal the clarity that has been long sought. When intuition leads to closure, pay attention to what it has to say. Your inner knowing is wise.

November 22

WITH A BULL'S-EYE AS THE TARGET, an archer aims their bow, slows their breathing, and releases. The arrow flies through the air as an arc, eventually hitting the mark. Sagittarians shows us that staying focused on a vision brings success. It's easy to get distracted when a goal seems far away. When there is a goal in sight, think of the archer and how they slow down, focus, and then act. It's a great example of follow-through. Appreciate the adventurous and focused Sagittarius in your life.

November 23

A SEEKER KNOWS that they don't have all the answers. Asking questions to gain understanding helps you grow in wisdom. There is no end to a seeker's pursuit, for one answer often leads to another question. Living life from this perspective is humbling. Curiosity shows us how much we have yet to know and appreciate the vast knowledge available. Analysis paralysis can also lead to inaction. When there is a goal at hand, seek the answers and remember to act.

November 24

FAMILIES CAN BE A PLACE of comfort but also distress. We can feel nurtured by our families and also misunderstood. Noticing where our needs aren't being met by our family can be a heartache and also a place of growth. Learning to nurture ourselves and finding a chosen family through friends and mentors can be quite healing. Seeking other relationships that meet our needs helps us to accept family members as they are. As healing occurs our expectations can transform into acceptance.

November 25

WHEN EVERYTHING SURROUNDING YOU FEELS CHAOTIC, you can always come back to your breath. Taking deep inhales and long exhales can soothe your nervous system when life feels frantic. Even if the situation feels like the chaos is endless, your breath is an anchor to lead you back to calm. Even if it's for just a moment, there is a grounding energy when we remember to breathe. Take a few deep breaths when chaos threatens your peace.

November 26

AS THE TREES RELEASE THEIR FINAL LEAVES, we are reminded to release all the things that no longer serve a purpose in our lives. What once may have worked, may be old news or an expired connection. Allow for a soulful release and see each thing as a leaf falling from the branches of your heart. Acknowledge any sorrow that comes up as you let go. Let the tears create space for what's to come when the timing is right.

November 27

RECOVERING IS A SPIRITUAL PRACTICE. At times it's difficult but often needed. Healing takes time as wounds become scars, reminders of restoration. You are not broken. Learning how to live from a new place of being and understanding is courageous. We can surprise ourselves when we access our inner strength. As you find your bearings on this new ground, breathe in the joy of healing and moving on. Affirm your fortitude and determination.

———

November 28

LIVING IN A LIMINAL SPACE is difficult. It's the time between what was and what's meant to be. Try to focus on the things that are happening right now and surrender all the desires that keep your heart from being present. Take a deep breath. Be patient. What's meant for you will happen. Sometimes letting go is what needs to happen so we can receive what's on its way. Most of the time it shows up when we least expect it.

November 29

WHEN WE RUSH THROUGH OUR DAYS, it's easy to lose track of time. Our minds are constantly one step ahead of our bodies and the present moment goes unnoticed. We miss the tiny moments that stir gratitude when we fly through life on autopilot. When you notice yourself mentally tripping over your to-do list, seek slow. Reject the urge to rush and breathe deeply. Take things one step at a time as you embrace the cadence of slowness.

———

November 30

SILENCE CALMS THE NERVOUS SYSTEM and helps us sink into the natural rhythms of sleep and wakefulness. When we spend our days hyperconnected in front of screens and artificial lights, our bodies forget their cyclical nature. Noise disrupts our thoughts and can keep us awake. Take time to seek silence by going for a walk or sitting alone at home. Find a way to welcome nothingness and let everything slip away. Soon you will enjoy the insights that silence provides.

December 1

AS YOU REFLECT ON THIS YEAR'S JOURNEY, repeat these affirmations to yourself: *I am grateful for the power of reflection. Looking back highlights lessons learned and joy-filled moments. Gratitude fills my heart as I look back on memories. I honor each moment shared, connection made, and wisdom gained. I am proud of myself for another year of growth. Deeper understanding has allowed me to release what no longer serves me and embrace what is meant to be. I look forward with hope, acknowledging that reflection allows hope to stay alive and thrive.*

December 2

LIFE IS ALL ABOUT SEASONS and their cyclical nature. Sometimes life is exciting, and opportunities seem to appear effortlessly. Other times we are called to what a Zen proverb refers to as "chop wood, carry water." During these times, it's the daily tasks and the gradual results of showing up that are important. In due time, life cycles back and the routines and tasks create times of excitement and rest. Celebrate your accomplishments, big and small, with gratitude when each cycle comes to an end.

December 3

MEMORIES OF LOVED ONES who have passed away are treasures. Being able to recall a special time with someone can brighten up a day. Our fond memories are proof of the deep connections in life. Even though it's hard to miss their presence, their memories live on. Honor these loving reminders by pausing when they arise. Feel the love and joy in your heart as you remember. Offer gratitude for the time you had with them and that their memory lives on within you.

December 4

SURRENDER AND PATIENCE ARE ESSENTIAL to moving forward. Eventually a renewed clarity will appear as time heals. We don't lose ourselves in loss, we grow through it. When we learn to release the tight grip on what we believe must happen, we open up to flourishing. Grief provides a period of tumult, like an abundant and extended rainstorm. Soon random patterns of growth and color pop up. Growth isn't linear and with that understanding, we can move forward with more compassion and gentleness.

December 5

MENDING A RELATIONSHIP takes time. Forgiveness is a choice that isn't always easy to make. When trust is broken, time tells us if the relationship is worth mending or moving on from. If you are the one who caused the hurt, show up consistently and apologize with words and actions. If you've been hurt and want to mend the relationship, stay open to the healing process. Take your time to restore what's been broken. Slowly, with effort and consideration, we can learn to trust again.

December 6

RIGHT BEFORE THE SUN SETS behind a mountain range, there is a pause. The final glimpse of the sun is a sacred moment, marking the end of another day. In this pause, we can think of something wonderful that occurred that day and offer gratitude for this beautiful moment in nature. Gratitude is available anytime, anywhere. Take a sacred pause and allow yourself to sink into the messages of your soul. Recount the goodness in your life and breathe in this momentary stillness.

December 7

CREATIVITY COMES IN MANY FORMS. Everyone is creative. No matter what the medium is, each of us is here with specific talents. It can feel scary to share our gifts with others, but not all creativity is meant to be shared. There is satisfaction in creating just for the sake of it. Your talent is as unique as your fingerprint and is part of the magic of who you are. When we celebrate the creative energy within, appreciation for ourselves and others grows.

December 8

WANDERING THROUGH A NEW CITY without a plan opens our minds and eyes to serendipity. Moving about aimlessly is an intentional way to invite magic into your day. Hidden gems are all over when we aren't looking for them. Lovely sights, delicious food, and friendly conversations are waiting to be discovered. Think about a time you've wandered. Recall some of the unexpected joys that happened along the way. Remember what it feels like to release expectations and open up to unexpected joy.

December 9

THE SUN RADIATES ENERGY, even after it sets. As our planet rotates, we still feel the benefits of the sun's powerful rays. Seasons remind us of our proximity to the sun as days become cooler or warmer. Even when we aren't around, we radiate energy toward the people in our lives. Notice how you feel after you see someone. Their energy is still radiating, leaving us feeling energized or drained. Take time to recharge as needed. Choose where you spend and emit your energy with care.

December 10

AS THINGS CHANGE energy starts to shift. Things that felt like weights begin to produce strength. Tunnels that seemed dark begin to illuminate with perspective. Tears that felt endless watered the seeds of the path you find yourself on. Hope is the balm that soothes heartaches. New beginnings look different than expected. Accept the changes and expand. Look at the horizon with this newfound hope. See everything with new eyes. All is well.

December 11

AS WE AGE we become more of ourselves. It's like a homecoming after years of trying on personas. We get more comfortable saying no to things that drain us and yes to things that renew us. Aging is a privilege and can be a joy. Gratitude helps us embrace this perspective as we fill our hearts and minds with all the things we are grateful for. Each day and age are a gift and there are so many magical moments to pause and give thanks for.

December 12

LIFE IS UNPREDICTABLE. We can feel like we have everything figured out and then something happens to challenge life as we know it. When these things happen, finding a way to settle your nervous system is important. Taking deep breaths can calm and ground a nervous heart. Check in with your breath. Are you holding it? Breathe in, filling your belly and chest. Hold for a moment and then exhale nice and long, even audibly, to release tension. Your breath is always available to you.

December 13

WHEN THE DAYS ARE SHORTER, there is often a pull inward. Pausing midday can add some much-needed peace into your schedule. Naps are a wonderful way to show yourself some care and love. Pushing through exhaustion when you need rest ignores a physical need. Naps can be as short as twenty minutes to refresh your mind and body. They are an act of kindness that you can give yourself often. Give yourself permission to take care of yourself.

December 14

ASSUMPTIONS CAN KEEP US FROM INTIMACY. When we assume something about another person, our judgments can keep us from digging deeper and knowing their truth. It's easy to speculate based on our past experiences. We project our thoughts on others, which at times keeps them at arm's length. Get curious when these assumptions arise. Reach out and ask questions. Try to be generous with your thoughts and give others the benefit of the doubt. They just may surprise you.

December 15

WHEN THINGS CHANGE it can be hard to adjust. We want things to stay the same, but we also know that's not possible. We can be attached to someone being a certain way, and the truth is we all grow and change every day. Release the desire for everything to stay frozen in time. Let the ice melt around this perfect vision and see how beautiful things are when we let life take its course and allow change to occur.

December 16

ANGER IS A MESSENGER from deep within our souls. It tells us when something isn't right, when boundaries are crossed, and when hurt occurs. Anger is a gift if managed well. Listen to its messages and take time to sort them out. Don't allow it to stew for too long, creating resentment; work through it. When it comes with a message, thank it for letting you know something is off, process it, and then send it on its way.

———

December 17

HEALING THE PAST comes from a compassionate approach to what happened to gain understanding. We may not be able to change the past, but we can learn how to pay attention to the wisdom our bodies hold. The body remembers much more than our minds. Through help from trained professionals and the loving connections in our lives, we can forge the path toward healing. Approaching the past with perspective and understanding can heal broken hearts and repair connections.

December 18

WHEN IT FEELS LIKE you've done everything to make something work and it still doesn't work out, take time to allow things to settle. Living in a state of constantly striving for perfection causes worry to bubble up. Fear peeks around the corner during these times of stress. When fear pops up, the need to control kicks in. However, taking a much-needed pause can help us find the redirection needed to move forward. In time, clarity has the space to appear.

———

December 19

UNEXPLORED GRIEF COMES UP when we least expect it. When we neglect our feelings by pushing them down, a wall is built around our soul. We block the beautiful flow that emotions provide as they move energy through us. Our past pain produces triggers and reactions. When we explore our pain, we can heal the wound. Grief is difficult to bear, and yet, resilience and acceptance spring forth from the softening it provides. Find someone to help you alchemize the grief so healing can occur.

December 20

THE WINTER SOLSTICE IS A TIME when light begins to return after the days have become shorter in length. As the temperatures continue to drop, we are called to get warm and cozy. Our homes provide a space to retreat to when the weather is cooler. This weather is only for a season. The daylight is lengthening and the sun will warm the earth once more. Recognize the fleeting nature of each season, embracing all this current one has to offer.

December 21

IT TAKES DETERMINATION TO CLIMB a mountain. A goat balances on the narrow trails and shaky rocks as it scales the peak, one step at a time. Its commitment to completing the task is discipline in action. Focusing on the greater goal, a Capricorn is able to lead a family or group to success. This example helps us see that when faced with a challenge, taking it one step at a time leads to victory. Appreciate the determined and committed Capricorn in your life.

December 22

HAVING A GOAL IS IMPORTANT when moving forward in life. However, being too attached to an outcome can hinder the ability to see other opportunities. At times the goal is just a guidepost to get us moving in the right direction. Along the way, we gain wisdom and occasionally plans change. Be open and flexible. Sometimes we meet a fork in the road that wasn't planned and we need to leave the planned path to find our purpose.

December 23

LEARNING TO LOVE AGAIN after loss can cause feelings of guilt to arise. Guilt is feeling that we did something wrong. Offer compassion here and remember that our hearts are meant to love and connect. Allowing your heart to open again after loss is an act of bravery and love. It's not easy to open up after loss. Be gentle with yourself and remember that we are all meant to seek connection. Release the guilt, and embrace love.

December 24

HIGH IN THE MOUNTAINS, snow insulates sound. There is a hush in the air that envelops nature. Everything feels serene and calm. When a disruption occurs, snow breaks from the mountain and tumbles down, causing an avalanche. This rapid slide can be very dangerous and brought on by disruptions. When life is disrupted, frustrations can create an avalanche of discontent. Notice the rising frustration and breathe slowly. Mindful awareness is the first step to settling rushing emotions and finding calm.

———

December 25

THE PRESENT MOMENT OFFERS us a gift to let go of the worries and thoughts that keep us from being here right now. This moment is all that matters. Gifts are not earned; they are given to the recipient without expectation. This moment was given to you, and you don't need to do anything to be worthy of it. You can put down the striving, comparison, and anxiety and receive the goodness of this day. Release a little with each breath. Receive this moment with gratitude and delight.

December 26

GRIEF IS LIKE A FINE DUST covering the heart. Even after time heals and moving on occurs, there are moments of remembrance that stir up the fine dust of grief. The smallest particles never seem to go away. What may have felt like a serene day can bring on tears through a memory. Grief lives in our hearts and stays as a reminder of the capacity it has for love. When it is stirred up, you've honored what was once loved. Eventually the dust settles and the ability to dream returns.

December 27

A TREE THAT ONCE SEEMED DEAD was merely dormant. After seasons of budding, flowering, and bearing fruit, a tree releases its leaves to rest. During winter, the tree stands barren, a stark contrast to its former crown of lush leaves. Nature offers this reminder that rest is important after producing. Soon enough spring will thaw the frozen branches and buds will begin to form, fruit will come, and all will be revealed. Until then, breathe deep and rest.

December 28

WHILE THE SUN DESCENDS, it casts a rose-gold glow on city buildings that reflect the day's final light. Palm trees stand tall in the sun's golden spotlight, glowing in warm glory. Sunsets seem to make everything radiant for a brief while. And then twilight occurs, and the memory of the glowing radiance dissipates. Memories are like the sunset; they come and go. When they appear, revel in their sweet reminders with gratitude.

December 29

THERE IS A SPACE WHERE CONNECTION HEALS, and the relationship is equal parts give and take. This is a rich place to be. It's the space where symbiosis occurs. Hold on to these energy-giving relationships where both parties feel refreshed after time together. Spend time where understanding and compassion thrive. Honor others' time as they honor yours. Celebrate and appreciate the people in your life who see and accept you for who you are.

December 30

BE COMPASSIONATE WITH YOURSELF. Life isn't fair. It's
full of hardship and pain. You are not alone when you feel
like things are hard. Part of offering yourself compassion is
recognizing that everyone has hard times. Be gentle with
yourself if you think you should be farther along from where
you are. Allowing comparisons to take over will only drag
you farther down. Becoming aware of when you need to be
more gracious with yourself opens the door to acceptance.

December 31

AS THE YEAR COMES TO AN END, reflect on the gratitude
you cultivated. Note how you began the year and everything
that has transpired. Take some time to journal about the
following questions: What celebrations have I experienced?
How have I changed? What most surprised me this year?
Continue to welcome gratitude each day and notice how
your heart and mind change as you calibrate them toward
appreciation. With daily gratitude, we honor our resilience
and growth and unlock the capacity for hope to thrive.

Acknowledgments

Many thanks to my publisher, Rage Kindelsperger. Your trust in my writing has changed my life. Thank you for taking time to listen to my ideas and for your mentorship over the years.

To my editors, Keyla Pizarro-Hernández and Cara Donaldson, I feel so lucky to have your care and corrections over my work. Thank you for knowing my voice and elevating my writing. I love how beautiful my books turn out and it's all because of the amazing Laura Drew, Kim Winscher, and the Quarto design team. Thank you to SpaceFrog Designs for another beautiful cover!

To my husband, Nate, I honestly don't have enough words to express how grateful I am for your patient love over the past several years. Thank you for being my biggest fan and for your never-ending love and belief in my work.

Thank you to my fellow author friends, Sarah Gregg, Lynn Haraldson, and Danielle Tantone for reading my writing and listening to these ideas when they were in their incubation stages.

Thank you to my family and friends who wrote cards, sent texts, and showed up during this difficult season.

I'm grateful for Dr. Stacy Hulley and her compassion and help to find the answers I was seeking. She is an angel on Earth in a health care system that leaves many women wondering what's wrong with them.

Therapy is a lifesaver and I'm grateful to Dana Pasculescu AMFT and Caron Collins LMFT for helping me walk through the valley of grief with perspective, useful tools, and compassion.

Going through infertility is tough; if you or anyone you know is struggling with infertility, resolve.org is an amazing resource and support. To the RESOLVE Community: Please see the September 6th passage on page 142 for a special reflection.

Author's Note

This book has been working its way through me for a few years. In January of 2020, I received the news that my dream of having a child would never come true. As the news settled in, I felt my soul slump. Grief took the place of hope, and my desire to create life turned into creating sentences.

It took a few years before I felt the buoyancy of hope beginning to return and ready to create and share again. Although this book was born through the grief of infertility, it addresses many of life's struggles. I wrote it with the intention to hold a candle for you when life seems dark. You are not alone.

About the Author

Emily Silva quit her corporate job in 2014 to pursue her dreams of becoming an author and starting her own business. She launched a coaching company that specializes in helping women harness their bravery to bring their gifts into the world. She helps her clients with midcareer changes and cultivating their spiritual lives. She lives with her husband in San Diego.

Emily is the author of *Moonlight Gratitude*, *Find Your Glow*, *Feed Your Soul*, *Sunrise Gratitude*, and *Moonlight Gratitude: A Journal*. To learn more, visit her website soulsadventures.com and follow her on Instagram at @soulsadventures.

First published in 2024 by Rock Point, an imprint of The Quarto Group,
142 West 36th Street, 4th Floor, New York, NY 10018, USA
T (212) 779-4972 www.Quarto.com

Rock Point titles are also available at discount for retail, wholesale, promotional, and bulk purchase.
For details, contact the Special Sales Manager by email at specialsales@quarto.com or by mail at The
Quarto Group, Attn: Special Sales Manager, 100 Cummings Center Suite 265D, Beverly, MA 01915 USA.

10 9 8 7 6 5 4 3 2 1

ISBN: 978-1-57715-428-0

Digital edition published in 2024
eISBN: 978-0-7603-8886-0

Library of Congress Cataloging-in-Publication Data
Names: Silva, Emily, author.
Title: Sunset gratitude : 365 hopeful meditations for peaceful and
   reflective evenings all year long / by Emily Silva.
Description: New York : Rock Point, [2024] | Summary: "Sunset Gratitude
   offers a collection of 365 thoughtful meditations to encourage you to
   have joyous evenings"-- Provided by publisher.
Identifiers: LCCN 2024006031 (print) | LCCN 2024006032 (ebook) | ISBN
   9781577154280 (hardcover) | ISBN 9780760388860 (ebook)
Subjects: LCSH: Gratitude--Miscellanea.
Classification: LCC BJ1533.G8 S553 2024 (print) | LCC BJ1533.G8 (ebook) |
   DDC 179/.9--dc23/eng/20240315
LC record available at https://lccn.loc.gov/2024006031
LC ebook record available at https://lccn.loc.gov/2024006032

Group Publisher: Rage Kindelsperger
Editorial Director: Erin Canning
Creative Director: Laura Drew
Managing Editor: Cara Donaldson
Editor: Keyla Pizarro-Hernández
Interior Design: Kim Winscher
Cover Illustration: @spacefrogdesigns

Printed in China

This book provides general information on various widely known and widely accepted images that tend
to evoke feelings of strength and confidence. However, it should not be relied upon as recommending or
promoting any specific diagnosis or method of treatment for a particular condition, and it is not intended as
a substitute for medical or mental health advice or for direct diagnosis and treatment of a medical or mental
health condition by a qualified physician. Readers who have questions about a particular condition, possible
treatments for that condition, or possible reactions from the condition or its treatment should consult a
physician or other qualified health care professional.